**ACPL ITEM
DISCARDED**

D1571834

5-27-75

Psyching Out Sex

Psyching Out Sex

INGRID RIMLAND

THE WESTMINSTER PRESS
PHILADELPHIA

COPYRIGHT © 1975 THE WESTMINSTER PRESS

All rights reserved—no part of this book may be repro-
duced in any form without permission in writing from
the publisher, except by a reviewer who wishes to
quote brief passages in connection with a review in
magazine or newspaper.

PUBLISHED BY THE WESTMINSTER PRESS ®
PHILADELPHIA, PENNSYLVANIA

PRINTED IN THE UNITED STATES OF AMERICA

Library of Congress Cataloging in Publication Data

Rimland, Ingrid, 1936–
  Psyching out sex.

  SUMMARY: Explores the joys and aches of sexual
loving from an emotional, rather than a physiological,
point of view.
  1. Youth—Sexual behavior. 2. Sex instruction for
youth. 3. Sex (Psychology) 4. Love. [1. Sex
instruction for youth. 2. Love] I. Title.
[DNLM: 1. Sex behavior—In adolescence. R576p HQ35]
HQ27.R55   301.41'07   74–26537
ISBN 0–664–20724–3
ISBN 0–664–24815–2 (pbk.)

1858450

CONTENTS

FOREWORD

Dealing as I do with young people every day, I have often felt the need for an informal, readable book that would raise some logical questions about things we take for granted in the realm of sexual loving. Therefore, PSYCHING OUT SEX was structured to contain a dozen informal chapters about the joys and aches of sexual loving: of the push behind human sexuality, of body image, of "love with a question mark." It talks about male needs for "blast offs" and male fears of "power failures," and speculates on the emotional reasons behind the seemingly slower female fuse. It takes a critical look at our finger-shaking culture and asks: "Conviction or habituation?" It talks about gentleness as well as savage hurting, both in the name of sexual love. It looks at the *results* of careless loving: at "accidental" babies born into an overcrowded world. It permits the reader to feel some of the convulsions brought about by unconventional sexual thinking, as many women shed their "chains" and many gays "take off their masks." Finally, it takes a peek at sex in tomorrow's world, leaving the reader with the feeling that vastly more might be asked of the sexual self than conventional know-how would have us believe.

This book has undergone several revisions with the assistance of half a dozen zestful anonymous teen-agers in my neighborhood who served as critics and judges of the manuscript as it developed. Their comments were very perceptive, always helpful, and very much to the point. They changed the flavor of an initial draft meant to impart rather conventional, widely agreed upon psychological principles to content designed to be novel and provocative for readers with intelligent, open, inquisitive young minds. Although this book touches on many facets of quite sophisticated psychological thinking, they wanted it simple in approach and easy to absorb. These kids drifting in and out of my office inquiring about "that deal you're writing" made me see that it should be written for smooth readability rather than scientific exactness, that it was more expedient to aim for overall scope rather than fine definitive distinctions. They made it quite plain that its professed goal should be challenge rather than absolute wisdom from "authority."

Thus, PSYCHING OUT SEX was written for a readership that craves some inner substance, that wants to know more than just assembly-line answers when temptation is pressing and hard to resist. It is meant to question and challenge in the light of current psychological thinking. It imparts some knowledge about the workings and wheels and fuels of the inner self in a language that young, imaginative readers can integrate into their often turbulent lives, so whatever emotions are felt and perceived will make a little better sense.

1

GENERATIONS ASKEW

An Introduction

Others tell us that we as people of a Western country seem addicted to sex. Sex is all around us—on the screen, in books, in magazines, in our language, our songs, and our behavior. We think, write, fantasize, and talk about sex. We joke about it, tease each other endlessly in veiled sexual hints, weep over disappointed sexual dreams, and sometimes even kill for it. Of such intensity is our preoccupation with the sexual act—by which we usually mean intercourse between two people of the opposite sex—that one would think us masters in the interpretation, the *meaning,* of sexual love.

Yet what is known of the inner sources by which people live sexually? What holds our fascination and fuels our preoccupation with the sexual act? What are the forces that make us go after sex with all our might or shy away from it as if our very soul could be scorched by sex that is forbidden?

Sex seems like a blank canvas on which many different shades of emotions can be artistically painted or thoughtlessly splashed. Tenderness, warmth, thoughtfulness, anger, shame, impotence, disappointment, loneliness, and many other aspects of our inner being can be portrayed on this canvas—in different hues and tints of feelings. Especially the magic and wonder that come with first sex can be bewitching in brilliance and shattering in fragility. Young people learn early how to have sex—they need to know what it *means* to have sex.

Opinions on the "true" meaning of sex will differ across the generation gap because the options today are different from what they were before. Today's young people cannot escape making very personal decisions regarding sex, and their parents cannot make these decisions for them. Some girls say they can no longer use fear of pregnancy as an excuse for *not* having sex. Birth control pills and other methods of contraception are freely available to teen-agers. So is abortion. The fear of pregnancy—if it ever worked at all to keep some girls from having intercourse—is less frightening today. Students drive cars that provide love nests and transportation to love nests. Motel operators act as if unmarried money is as good as married money. Mixed dormitories in many colleges—and relaxed rules as to when girls must be in their rooms—mean that brick walls and brass locks are no longer the barriers they once were. Many unmarried couples rent apartments and set up housekeeping together. Even during high school years, students are likely to know some very clean-cut, intelligent, scholastically successful, socially conscious classmates and campus leaders who make no great attempts to hide their social unions. The time is past when parents maintained physical control over their daughters by having chaperones around who would watch couples so that they could never have a chance to be alone together. A generation or two ago, it may have been only "loose" or "easy" girls who confessed to a sexual appetite. When grandparents were young and in love, they may have been concerned about whether a little good-night kiss was proper on a first date, and parents may have been worried as to where the boundaries between "light" and "heavy" petting should be. Today's generation is more often frankly concerned about whether to go to bed and when.

Today's young people must be guided by their own choices and values and beliefs—and not by locks and chaperones and brick walls—as to what sort of life to live sexually. Parents may try to shut their eyes and pretend that their children do not face such choices, do not know anything about sex, do not have any sexual opportunities or thoughts, but this does not change the facts.

Therefore many parents are now faced with the painful task of having to look at a lifetime of values they held dear and recognize their own lack of freedom in the sexual realm. It is not always easy to look at one's convictions as coolly as one should. Parents still find it painfully difficult to tell their boys and girls about the simplest facts of life— with the result that young people are sometimes left with lifelong psychic wounds that perhaps would not need to have been inflicted. Many psychosexual problems are man-made problems, arising out of the way we feel about our bodies, our natural drives, and our sexual "misdeeds."

Many people feel and act as if sex were just a matter of

a physical performance that can be perfected by "knowing which buttons to press." Many marriage and sex manuals contain pages and pages about technical know-how: what a penis or a vagina looks like, how sperm gets from the man's testicles to the woman's ovum, what causes menstruation, and how babies grow in the uterus—but contain little about what sex *means* to people, or how it *feels*. The physical basis of sexual intercourse—that part of sex which even children can most easily understand—is important, of course. But much more relevant is the emotional, the psychological, the *feelingful* side of sex. We cannot show pictures or charts of exactly how sex feels and what it means; but the things we can't diagram are important, too.

Sex means having access to the innermost world of another human being. When two people are attracted to each other, it seems natural that they would want to be close— as close as possible, physically and emotionally. They want to touch, to hold, to have contact. One of the most beautiful things about sex is that it is a way of saying without words: "I like you. It seems right with you. You seem nice and attractive to me. It's fun to be together with you. I enjoy lying here close to you, with our naked bodies snuggled up so tightly together this way. No one else can ever take the place of you and me and re-create exactly the same feelings we are sharing together right now." Sex is fellowship, friendship, emotional closeness. Precisely because intercourse is carried out in privacy, it is a way of excluding the rest of the world and sharing a special intimacy with a very special friend. Children and grown-up children enjoy sharing a secret, and slipping off one's clothes is a way of sharing secret parts and sights and feelings. Clothes are a symbol of the fronts, the pretenses, the facades we must wear as we face a critical, cold, often angry world. Taking off one's clothes can be a way of dropping one's pretenses and becoming more open with another person we genuinely like.

Many people go through the mechanical procedures of intercourse without experiencing this intimacy and openness and fellowship that sex can bring. They may be so embarrassed that they cannot talk, or so guilty over violating conscience that they cannot lift their heads, or so angry over having been seduced that they cannot be friendly.

This is, young voices now insist, because such lovers have inherited a burden of sexual taboos, taboos for which the older generation feels forced to take the blame. Many young people strongly insist that the rules regarding premarital sex will have to be rewritten. The young point out that there are many decent ways to chart one's course into responsible sexual adulthood, and having had experience before marriage, they feel, is not necessarily the liability their parents often think it is.

"Right is right, and wrong is wrong," says Father. "What about decency, and self-respect, and responsibility? What about babies that are born as a result of casual sex—children nobody wants or needs? What about the feelings of others who are hurt by careless sexual conduct?" And Mother, aching that suddenly virginity should be a mockery, asks, "What about love?"

In our Western world, we talk about a sexual relationship with another person as "loving" that person, but of course it is possible to have sex without love. Love between a man and a woman is a psychological matter that may or may not result in the physiological expression of intercourse. It is one of the characteristics of our culture to think that love and sex go naturally together in some way. Sometimes this will happen, and sometimes it does not; we can enrich the scope of our emotional awareness by understanding emotionally as well as intellectually that love does not always precede sex, just as marriage does not always precede intercourse. Our Western culture has decreed that this *should* be so, and much heartbreak and disillusionment comes from this expectancy. At its best, sex can be a wonderful expression of what we think of as love, because the word "love" means many things: tenderness, kindness, unselfishness, self-acceptance, responsibility, warmth, closeness, and so on. It may also mean—as we will see when we take "love" under scrutiny—things that aren't so noble and nice.

Young people seem to perceive this to a degree. Love, for them, has broadened; it is no longer as tightly tied to sex and one person alone. Books, television, and the motion picture screen are making very plain that cultural answers as to what is right and what is wrong have changed in the past and across countries and continents and are likely to change again in the future. Precut, prefabricated cultural answers may therefore be less than adequate in satisfying young people today. At a time in their lives when sexual wishes become the source of upheaving and often frightening emotions, choice about sexual conduct will have to be made with better assistance than a cultural measuring rod marked "right" and "wrong."

This book offers an alternative: a kaleidoscopic means of looking at sex in terms of the emotional costs and rewards of intercourse. It would be dishonest and incorrect to take the moral stance that there are no rewards; the rewards of sex—forbidden or not—can be very sweet indeed. But there are also costs: to oneself, one's partner, one's parents, one's family and friends, and finally the society into which one has to fit. Sexual enjoyment can't always be had for the asking. Sex, too, may have its price tag—to be paid in psychological coin.

This is a candidly written book. It does not speak for or against a particular code of sexual behavior. Readers can and must make their own decisions. They can make these decisions more wisely if they are equipped with knowledge about sex, especially its psychological aspects. It can be anticipated that some readers will be openly and frankly engaged in sexual relations with a partner to whom they are not married, and that others will be deeply committed to the belief that sex is only for the married. That is a matter of individual choice. Our choices, however, as we will see, are influenced by many things.

This book attempts to show how such a choice may come about, or may have come about in the past. Psychology tells us that, to a large extent, our inner sense of well-being—our emotional comfort—depends on our ability to see ourselves as emotionally constructed in an orderly way. We seem to lack the psychological equipment to deal with too many "ifs" and "buts" in our beliefs. We hurt from clashing contradictory emotions. We don't like to be at odds with ourselves. If we do declare war on ourselves—as frequently happens when sex is involved—we go to extraordinary lengths to protect our inner world.

The following chapters should help readers to see some order and regularity in what they think and do sexually, so that they may understand some of the powerful feelings

involved in sexuality. It is hoped that this book will help
them to bring to their sexual roles the deeper sense of
awareness that lends confidence and surety to an artist's
brush.

2

FORCES SPINNING OUR WHEELS

The Question of Free Will

Young lovers behave, it is sometimes facetiously said, as if they were "moonstruck." Powerful influences "hit" people in love. Lovers are helpless, it seems. There are mysterious powers that make them act differently from the sane, normal, reasonable human beings they would otherwise be. Intuitively, we all believe in this. There's Cupid with his arrows at Valentine's, lying in wait for his "victims." We speak of "falling in love" as if falling into an abyss. "I couldn't help myself," parents are often glowingly or tearfully told. "I don't know what came over me."

Do emotions have power over behavior? Does being in love dictate our wish to have intercourse and what we do about fulfilling that need? If so, are we then really free to say no to a temptation? If there is a relationship between being in love and having sex, and if one causes the other, then it would seem logical to think that the more we love a person, the stronger will be our push for sex, and the weaker will be our freedom to say no.

Just how much freedom of choice is there, according to present psychological knowledge?

One school of thought says there is none. According to one psychological theory, free will is an illusion.

Behaviorists have this to say:

Just as there are laws directing the universe, there are laws directing behavior. And just as there is order and prediction in the physical world from the motions of the molecules to the movements of the galaxies, there is order and prediction in what human beings do. Man's behavior is controlled by pleasure experienced and pain avoided. Man will move to seek pleasure, and he will move to avoid pain. All rewards are pleasure. All punishments are pain. Pleasure and pain may be both physical and psychological. Sex may be pleasurable physically but painful psychologically, or vice versa, or all pleasure, or mostly pain, or a little bit of each. How man reacts to sex—whether he will approach it or avoid it—depends on how he has experienced it *before:* what the ingredients of sexual experience and learning were from earliest childhood on.

According to this school of thought, it is erroneous to talk about "wishes" and "motives" and "needs" and "resolutions" as if they were entities having power over one's actions. We may be experiencing a sensation we call love, but it is wrong to say that it is love that dictates our behavior, just as it is wrong to ascribe an emotion to a falling rock. Before people came to understand the laws of gravity, they speculated that there was a "jubilance" in a falling body that *made* it speed up as it approached the earth. It is just as erroneous to think that it is love that causes us to have sex, or hate that makes us abandon our partner. It is pleasure experienced and pain avoided that is responsible for our sexual conduct, and not "love" or "lust" or "conscience" or "wishes" or "needs." Emotions are a by-product of our behavior; it is only because our understanding of ourselves is still so crude and simplistic that we ascribe the power of control to a sensation which happens to take place.

According to this theory, much of our so-called good or right behavior is nothing but psychological pain avoided by turning one's back on psychological stimuli that are taboo. Psychologists who adhere to the above school of thought are not concerned with questions about right or wrong—at least not in the sense of leaving this decision up to one's will power. They say that questions of right or wrong are irrelevant; if we want kids to be good, we should not ask them to be good and keep our fingers crossed and hope for the best. Instead, we should remove temptation or rearrange sexual learning. As long as sex is more pleasurable than painful, both in the physical and psychological sense, kids will keep on falling in love and not knowing what happened to them afterward.

To other psychologists, however, this line of thought is sheer heresy. Phenomenologists point out that human beings have—after all!—some *reasoning* faculties.

The sexual push may be there, but it can be ignored, or diverted, or postponed, or defused. We may be helpless to experience outrage, but we certainly don't need to kill a man. We cannot avoid experiencing hunger, but we can choose when to eat, and how much, and what, and with whom. We may have had an experience before that told us sex may be pleasurable, but we are at liberty to postpone intercourse until the time is right and the partner is right.

We can't help having occasional fantasies that are forbidden, but we can force ourselves to think of a sunset instead. At least to a degree we are free to sort out the acceptable from the forbidden and discard that which we don't like. There is a certain leeway in choosing one's behavior; *there is at least partial control.*

This school of thought supports the idea of separation of mind and body. Man's lower sexual needs are under the control of man's higher reasoning abilities. Man's personality is seen as a mixture of reason and emotion. These two parts of man's self are commonly perceived as being antagonistic toward each other: if reason wins, emotions lose out; if emotions get the upper hand, it will be at the expense of reason. Emotions may be powerful and may have to be kept in check; but we can always call upon our intellectual censor and control those emotions we do not like.

According to this theory, emotions are our behavioral energy. Desires, wishes, needs, and drives are the fuels that determine what we do. The relative strength of these emotions will decide what will happen sexually, and when, and with whom. Not only are we motivated, we are motivated in a certain direction which may be either toward or away from intercourse.

According to this theory, too, man is compelled to take steps to satisfy his sexual needs. But he does not do so helplessly, at the mercy of prior learning. He has his intellect: he filters his needs through a reasoning process and hereby gains control over them. Man's reason is the regulatory force that determines what he should do about his sexual needs.

Let's listen to some of these "reasoning" arguments:

"We learn by doing. Sexual learning, much like any

other learning, is a hit-or-miss affair—it is of a trial-and-error nature. Does it not then make more sense to place the emphasis on 'trial' rather than to grieve and lament over 'error'?''

\"But sex for experimentation means tinkering with man's most sensitive emotional machinery. Experimentation is by no means a guarantee for growth. Sexual intercourse is a sensitive act that involves the tapping of deepest inner feelings. Coming to love a person sexually is a slow and delicate process of growth, and nothing could possibly be gained by light and flippant behavior. One's own feelings are sacred territory. Sexual testing is frivolous.''

"Isn't a man-woman relationship one of the most complex and sensitive relationships a person is ever to enter? Why would one want to taboo preparation for such an important and lasting step? Emphasis in sexual experimentation could be on tenderness and affection as preparation for a successful marriage later on.''

"Rules have to be learned before one can understand the reasons behind these rules. Children learn traffic safety long before they are permitted to drive a car. They learn to keep hands off a box of matches long before they can grasp the dangers inherent in the misuse of fire. Teen-agers have to learn to respect sexual rules because there are great dangers in the misuse of sex.''

"However, peer attitudes are important to the young, and peer pressure works in favor of sex. Young people have to build self-esteem. They have to establish their sexual identity and verify their sexual role many times over before they can be comfortable with their sexual attributes. So does it not make sense to let them find out for themselves just what it is that is so mysterious and powerful? Sexual curi-

osity is part of growing up, and as such is sound psychological training ground. Adolescence, in many ways, is a transitory period: it is too early to marry and settle down, but it
is not too early to be aware of and to want to try out one's
machinery for sex. Young people have developmental
needs where sex could be very useful."

"But there is, after all, one's conscience. It acts as a
built-in gyroscope: all too easily can it spin out of balance
and make us very nauseous emotionally if we do that which
is not right. One's conscience is a reliable reference point
for making a sexual choice, because life can be very uncomfortable if one feels out of touch with one's beliefs. Therefore, there is a built-in reward in waiting for that special
person and saving oneself for a special relationship."

"Nevertheless, it seems absurd that people should be
asked to 'buy a pig in a bag'—to enter a relationship that is
supposed to last a lifetime without having sampled what
they are 'buying.' "

Reasoning arguments, it seems, are far from consistent
and safe.

Many psychological models have been constructed to
explain man's sexual self, man's war with himself and his
bodily cravings. The best-known model is that of Sigmund
Freud, the Viennese physician who, some people feel, had
more to say about sex and psychology than anyone before
his time or since.

In Freudian thinking, there are three parts to man's self:
the id, the ego, and the superego. The "villain" is the id;
this part of man consists mostly of sexual desires. It is,
however, not visible to outsiders; except for a very incon-
spicuous surface, it is submerged within the subconscious—
much like an iceberg, huge but unseen.

The superego is a name for man's conscience. It is a force that forbids man his sexual appetite. The superego is harsh, and strict, and relentless. It keeps watch over the "villain" so that no harm can be done. The id may strain and push from below, to no avail: man's conscience keeps watch over man's sexual drive and sees to it that it does not get out of hand.

Because the superego is such a strict policeman, and the id such a powerful villain, they need a mediating force: man's ego, the reality principle. The ego's role is that of go-between, getting the superego to be less strict and the id to be less sexually gluttonous. The ego is forever involved in bending and slanting sexual wishes so that they may be acceptable to the superego's specifications.

An example may be the ego's handling of man's exhibitionistic needs. Many men and boys are thought to have the hidden desire to show off their sexual genitals. Such a wish is most offensive and unacceptable to man's superego, so the ego compromises and gets man to wear and show off a tie instead, and both id and superego have their way. According to this model, the id is responsible for everything that we do, whether it is of a visibly sexual nature or not.

In infancy, the id is given free reign. Bodily cravings and demands for instant satisfaction are natural to very young children. As they grow up and learn to submit to societal rules and expectations, the superego is strengthened more and more, and sexual wishes are checked rigorously against the reality principle: are they acceptable to the superego, or not?

This model, of course, is only an artificial creation: a speculation as to man's sexual makeup. However, it is the best-known model that we have, and it is useful in that it can be applied in psychoanalysis, the repairing of one's psyche. By means of special clinical tools and techniques, man's hidden sexual energy is released and brought out into the open, so that it may be faced squarely and thereby lose some of its threatening properties.

This model affirms our intuitive belief that emotions are somehow not quite to be trusted. Emotions are forces that push below the surface, much like steam in a kettle, with conscience having to hold down the lid. And in no other area in life do emotions seem as suspect as in sex.

Why do we think emotions can't be trusted?

Emotions can be manipulated. They can be magnified by drugs. They can be wiped out by artificially created convulsions. They can be shaped to evil intentions by a process called brainwashing, by which clever words are used in such a way as to divert formerly held beliefs and ideals. Tiredness can make us grouchy and unfair with the person we love. We are not as likely to feel amorous on a full stomach, but candlelight may help. Alcohol gives emotions a giddy tinge, but classic music can make emotions very somber indeed.

Emotions are contagious: we can "catch" an emotional current from another person much like we can catch a cold. Have we not all found ourselves aching at times with laughter over things that may not be funny at all, just because others were laughing? And aren't there times when we will weep with others even though their sorrow may only lightly touch our sympathy? Could we not be "caught by love" against our will?

Some people speculate that just as our looks are fixed by our genetic heritage, nature has given us a blueprint of our emotional capacity and "normalcy." Folklore has long believed in this. An obese person is thought to be jolly. A redhead is suspected of a fiery temperament. Blond, blue-eyed girls are usually thought to be meek. Black curls are a "sure giveaway" of hidden sexual passions. The theory that body constellation and certain character traits go hand in hand found support some years ago through the discovery that the mass murderer Richard Speck was the carrier of an extra sexual chromosome. Speck slaughtered eight young student nurses in a single night in a Chicago apartment house. When caught by police, he was calm and relaxed and showed not the slightest sign of emotion. It was as if, within this man, feelings were severed from behavior: his emotions seemed not connected with what he had done.

Some, if not all, emotions are clearly tied to our body chemistry. Our body reacts to the presence of emotions in ways that can be measured and recorded. Emotions can make the lie detector's needle jump as the criminal is questioned on his deeds. His palms start to sweat. His skin tightens. His blood pressure increases. Suddenly his mouth goes dry. The body becomes a sensitive instrument that reacts involuntarily despite an attempt at deception.

The body reacts to emotions in everyday life as well.

> "Lisa would make me see red. . . . She would giggle and smile and tease me all through history class. I would start shaking whenever she was near; I had to try hard to keep my hands from trembling. I wanted desperately to ask her for a date, but when she looked at me this way, I felt that I was being choked."

Often, the more we try to suppress emotions, the more they push to be released. If some of the more serious emotions are blocked from expression, they may go into our bodily system and cause us to have rashes or ulcers or paralyze our limbs. Doctors have many stories to tell how emotions can turn "hostile" on the body that houses them.

Even our culture has something to say about emotions and how they are to be felt and expressed. Not all emotions are "created equal," by any means. Some are permitted expression, others are forced underground. Some are permitted free speech today and forbidden a voice tomorrow. We are forbidden to hate except the enemy during war; we are forbidden to love sexually except after the proper wedding bells have rung. Culture even decides on the proper vehicle for our emotions: sexual themes have free reign in music, are partially free in sculpture and art, are permitted a somewhat reluctant tongue-in-cheek existence on the *Playboy* centerfolds, and are zealously persecuted in anything resembling pornography.

Emotions—much like beauty—may be in the "eye of the beholder." Experiments have shown that how we feel about sex may determine just how much sexual stimuli we see. The word "sex" flashed briefly on a screen may be translated as "six" by a girl brought up to think that sex is equal to sin. By contrast, "six" may become "sex" for a boy who saw Linda Lovelace at the movies the night before and perhaps dreamed about her afterward. Emotions see to it that "innocent" stimuli become sexually charged. Emotions will also defuse sexual stimuli that are a threat to one's self.

In the light of the above, it would seem somewhat unreasonable to insist that young boys and girls are wholly and totally at liberty to say no to premarital sex. But neither are they at liberty to say yes. There are physical and psychological and cultural reasons that have a say in how we feel and what we do, some of these cues coming from within and some coming from the world in which we happen to live.

There are reasons why some emotions are acceptable and some are not, and why emotions are strong at times and weak or absent at others.

If there is a relationship between body chemistry and how loving or mean we feel at the moment, or between upbringing and how much sex we see, or between wrong-doing and soft music and candlelight, then we have to admit that much more is involved in a sexual choice than to depend on our "built-in radar" to tell us right from wrong.

Nor would it seem enough to stipulate that love should be present to sanctify sex. "Love" is the name for a specific package of emotions that make us see what we *expect* to see. Let's look at love.

3

THE CRYSTAL BALL

Love as a Psychological Construct

Love, we are convinced, means *giving*. Sex, we often believe, means *taking away*. At the same time, we think that love and sex go naturally together in some way. We often state that love between two people is basically sexual attraction, yet sex alone is never called love.

This chapter will examine this thing called "sexual love" and some of its many contradictions. It will highlight some attributes of sexual love as they are commonly understood by young people bewitched by an emotion that transforms perfectly ordinary young people into enticing, glowing, radiant human beings who flirt and kiss and neck and pet and very much want intercourse with the person with whom they are "in love."

When we think of love, we usually think of happiness. It seems easy to assume that everyone knows what happiness is. In our times, we usually think of happiness as having what we want: money, security, power, the respect of others, fashionable clothes, a new car, good grades, a date with the football hero or the beauty queen, sex on a secluded beach. Yet a wise man by the name of Diogenes who lived many centuries ago taught others that happiness meant living a life *free of wants.* To demonstrate his point, he lived in a tub on the outskirts of his town. Parents teach children that happiness means leading a self-disciplined life. The hippies and the flower children of not too many years ago believed that happiness meant living a life free of all responsibility. The Christian martyrs defined happiness as sacrifice: they chose to be killed by lions or they died nailed to a cross. Some Catholic nuns and priests have believed that happiness means suppressing all sexual thoughts and concentrating their wishes on a life after death. Many old people find happiness in bittersweet memories, reliving the times long past. Happiness is not an *absolute:* it can be many different things, according to how one looks at it. *Its nature is defined by our wishes and needs.*

So it is with sexual love. We have certain wishes and needs, we expect certain things when we speak of being "in love." These expectations dictate just what love should be like. In a way, love is a man-made creation. The word "love" is a mental tool, a label, a name we have given to an enchanting emotion we experience when we find ourselves attracted to a member of the opposite sex. It is an emotion with a specific focus, so to speak. When we think of love, we usually think of someone roughly equal to us in age, and, most of the time, our "love" will be good-looking, and charming, and good, and kind, and *perfect.* And sooner

or later—we hope—the target of our attraction will catch
the spark and love us in return. Once this is attained, "love"
will take care of the rest.

Or so we believe. We like to believe that love is always
constructive. If love goes awry, it is love "gone bad." We
do not seem to think that love may be destructive. This
seems to be the reason why we show tolerance and understanding for the jealous lover. A jealous person is forgiven
all kinds of destructive behavior because he acts, after all,
in the grip of a "double-crossed" love. Something sacred
has been violated. He is not expected to be in control of
himself, because his love has gone sour. He takes, as it were,
his disappointed feelings and wears them like a badge on his
sleeve that permits him irrational and hurtful behavior. We
much disapprove of a lover who takes a broken love relationship in stride. We feel he must not have loved the
genuine way. Love as an intellectual judgment is far more
puzzling to us than love as a wild-eyed obsession.

> "I was sitting with Pete at McDonald's when Don came
> stomping in. He gave me this *look*, you know. It made me
> freeze in my boots. I had not been sure about Don until
> then. I kind of liked Pete a lot; we had a lot in common. But
> that night I gave in to Don. I knew he loved me and I loved
> him. I realized it the moment he looked at me with that
> *expression* on his face."

Most of us believe sex is a part of love, with "Love"
capitalized, and sex somewhat bashful on its trail. There are
a few who feel that love should equal sex, and vice versa,
and others who are convinced that sexual wishes, being
"lowly" emotions, could never reach the lofty heights of
love. Most of us agree that love is *the* supreme emotion, and

that somehow sex has to be brought under the auspices of love. If it is sex and intercourse we want, we like to be *sure* that we are really and truly "in love."

When we adhere to this idealistic concept of love, we give it a *moral dimension.* This distinction between love and sex is made in terms of "caring about the other person as a person." We think that there is something less than dignified in sex unless we approve of the partner as an individual and not merely as a convenient mechanical device that helps us achieve sexual relief. We are fond of saying that we should love people and use things, and we feel guilty if we discover that there are times when we love things and use people.

The term "using a girl" means using her sexually for selfish ends. It has the ring of consumption without restitution. Our perception of love as a higher-order emotion does not permit us to be comfortable with having sex and intercourse with a partner unless we are psychologically involved —unless we "love" our partner, at least a tiny bit. Of course it is possible to have sex without love, but such experience is usually not very satisfying to either partner because they feel that they "took" and gave nothing in return. For intercourse to "feel right," a psychological involvement seems necessary.

This ingredient called "giving" is particular to sexual love. Our conscience lets us "consume" in other relationships. A student may take from a teacher for years without ever having to feel guilty about depleting this teacher by his selfishness. We don't usually think that a child will take too much of his mother's emotional resources. A child is *expected* to take, and a mother is *expected* to give. The same is true of a relationship between a priest and his parishioner, or a doctor and his patient, or a counselor and his counselee. Friends are expected to take from each other; indeed, this is what friendship is believed to be all about. Any love relationship that has no sexual overtones gives permission to take without giving. It is only when a person is sexually desired that consumption seems a less than noble wish. If we are comfortable at all in taking sexually, we do so only as an *exchange*.

Sexual love, we also believe, is *sudden*. Love, as an emotion, will break into full bloom overnight. We will "fall in love" and live happily ever after, because our movies tell us that we do, and sometimes powerful feelings make us think we do. This "striking of lightning," we believe, is the true and exclusive hallmark of sexual love.

With other emotions, however, we make no such demands. Do we "fall in friendship" with the same speed and under the same conditions and with the same fierceness? In friendship we make allowances for an infinite *range* of emotional involvement. We have casual friends, and good friends, and close friends, and best friends. We give our feelings time to grow and to develop, and we do our part to nurture them to healthier bloom. We grow toward and away from our friends, and we don't let our hearts be broken to quite the same extent if a friendship we held dear somehow dies on us.

Related to this expectation of suddenness is our belief that love has to be *permanent*. This is why it hurts so much when love comes and goes in what seems to be a moment's notice.

"Tom and I saw each other all summer long. Our folks were beginning to hear wedding bells. So did I, almost before I realized how deeply I was involved. I gave in to him for the first time after a drive-in movie to which we had gone. It seemed the natural thing to do. . . . I mean, it would not have seemed right not to have sex, for me to hold back. We had sex after that for a couple of nights, and then Tom stayed away. I don't know what happened . . . what I did wrong. I loved him so."

Girls seem to feel this hurt far more than boys. Boys have their reservations about everlasting love, for reasons which we will discuss in later chapters. Yet could it be that sexual love would be healthier if we could think of it as having a beginning and an end, with a certain life of its own in between, with a certain sequence and a certain order of progression? All human relationships seem transitory—sexual ones included. Because we have *defined* this emotion called love to be permanent, we expect it to be. Emotions feed on the existence of needs from which they spring, and if our needs should change, it would seem natural that we would want to shift our sexual interests in another direction. Yet if we change our sexual partners, we usually experience a bitter sense of loss.

This strange emotion called sexual love compels us to want *perfection.* We are in love with an idealistic concept of love. We make a sharp distinction between the loved one and other ordinary mortals. We are convinced that the person we love possesses every flattering attribute possible. We are astounded to discover that the world does not seem to see our partner as we do. We are convinced from the bottom of our hearts that our perception is right—the rest of the world simply lacks our sharpened insight. We are the only ones with clear vision.

"Mom thought Liz was a slut. She said she'd be a poor housekeeper, only concerned about herself and her looks, and that she was selfish and vain and had no manners. Of course I didn't listen. I was nuts about that chick. To me, she was the most beautiful thing in the world. . . . She had the most innocent smile and the sexiest pair of legs. She couldn't help but be perfect, I thought."

The lover forms an image of his ideal person, and then finds himself attracted to this picture he has created. By setting standards of perfection, he acts like the proverbial ostrich and pretends that imperfections do not exist. In a way, this is a form of self-deception. This denial of reality is common to people very much in love: a conscious attempt to shut out the rest of the world, to fight off even the suggestion of a less than perfect love. It means slanting intellectual information coming one's way to one's more pressing emotional needs. The outside information regarding "our" love has to filter through our emotions first and takes on the colors of our emotions.

Love is also commonly seen as springing from a *surplus* of emotions or as being a surplus of kindness that one shares. It may well be that this feeling called love springs from an emptiness or a need. Many theories of human behavior stress that people act because of inner needs. There is no theory as yet which says that people act from innate generosity. This is an important distinction, because if love is given from an inner surplus which is plentiful, it will be different in quality from love which is sought under duress. If our inner needs are such that we don't have a surplus from which to draw, asking us to "give" in a sexual relationship may be an impossible demand. It may mean depleting even more our emotional resources. There may be many times

1858450

when psychologically our needs may compel us to take rather than to give.

> "There was this guy named David who used to date my sister Sally. Girls simply flipped over him. And Sally is a knockout herself, as you know. He took her out for five weeks in a row, and she bragged about him at every turn. He never once bothered to look my way—he was totally shot on Sally. I made up my mind about him then. It was going to be David and no one else. I cornered him at the library one day, and I pretended to brush against him accidentally. I could tell by the look on his face he had finally noticed me. That night we had sex in his car, behind the Safeway Store on Douglass Street, while Sally was inside shopping for a picnic that she and Dave had planned for the weekend."

Another feature of this emotion called sexual love is that we believe it to be *exclusive.* We "know" that the attraction we feel for our partner is of such intensity that it would be impossible to duplicate it for anyone else in the world. It is as if by focusing our desire on only one person at one time we are making sure of the purity of our feelings. The sanctity of love itself seems threatened by the very thought of loving more than one person sexually. Yet in other emotions involving feelings of love, we put no such limits on our focus. A mother's love is seen as "pure," but she may love all six of her children equally. A teacher may well love thirty kids in the class. A humanitarian may find love for all mankind in his heart. The God of the Bible is believed to have an inexhaustible amount of love for all that is in heaven and on earth. But true sexual love, as we understand it, is for one and one person alone: "To love and to cherish, till death do us part." We seem to give a tiny inch when we allow for sexual love to occur for different partners in *succession,* but never at the same time. It is one of the sharpest taboos we have put around this concept called sexual love. It is the foundation on which our social structure is built. We would not have families, and homes in which children could grow up in relative safety, if we did not believe in love as *having to be* exclusive. It seems a worthwhile belief to hold.

Yet exclusive love may also give us permission for selfish behavior. It is not uncommon in sexual love to want to dominate the partner to the extent of having control over the partner's very thoughts. "Lovers have no secrets" is a commonly held belief, and a saying we take as an ideal. Lovers will often strive to be alike. Indeed, we think that lovers *should* be alike: in thoughts, in tastes, in interests, in outlook on life, in sexual preferences, and so on. There can be suffocation, however, in such closeness. Perhaps it could be asked if anyone has a right to "love" in such a narrow fashion. It seems to involve another person's right to inner privacy. The concept of autonomy is a very important principle of good mental health. It stresses an individual's right to have an inner world of his own making, an emotional territory where no one is allowed to intrude against his will.

We also think that love should be *unselfish,* that the partner's needs should always have preference over one's own. Yet a sexual relationship seems to have a large component of *narcissism*—being in love with oneself. This term is derived from the Greek legend of the boy Narcissus, who fell so deeply in love with his own image reflected in the still waters of a pond that he died of longing for that image which he could never possess. We often see in our partner that image of ourselves. This is a form of projection: we think of our partner as we would like the person to be, that is, *as we are.* In a way, it is narcissism in disguise. It may be more acceptable to love another person for the attributes we flatter ourselves to possess. Yet this is not loving the partner for what he is. It means loving the partner for what we would like him to be. We can make love very selfish by "helping" our partner to measure up to his "true" self.

And finally, let's look at the villain called "raw sex." When we disapprove of the hedonistic aspects of sex—of having sex for fun—we usually mean to say that fun is quite all right, but sex should be *more* than pleasure alone. This way, sex becomes a construct, too: a name we give to feelings that have to do with sexual behavior and intercourse. We give sex a *moral dimension,* just as we did when we defined love as being kind and good and constructive and sudden and permanent and so on. It is quite legitimate to say that there is more to sex than fun. But it is important to hold separate in our minds the act of sexual intercourse and the emotional attributes with which we adorn that act. We have a habit of adorning many things with attributes that have a moral dimension. We say that "work is good," that "self-denial helps us to grow," "sorrow will lead to victory," and so on. But these are value judgments that may or may not be true. They could be argued both ways. It is a value judgment to say that sex for pleasure only is a thing to be avoided. In other areas of life we condone pure pleasure-seeking behavior, such as in art, and in recreation, and in our preference of friends, and in travel, and in many other ways. We don't see pleasure-seeking behavior as wrong *unless* it is connected with sex.

In the following chapters, we will see how we have learned to hold certain expectancies and beliefs regarding the nature of love and sex. These expectancies are part and parcel of one's emotional makeup, the psychological "me." Regardless of how we have come to acquire them, they are very real to us. Since they are part of our psyche, they are to be respected, to be taken account of and reckoned with when we engage in sexual behavior. Underlying the chapters to come will be the premise that it will enrich the scope of our awareness to realize just how emotions surrounding sex can play havoc with our lives.

4

THE PLAYBOY IDEAL

Body Perception and Self

We have within ourselves a mental picture of ourselves—
of our own individual worth. This mental image is tied, at
least in part, to our perception of our body: whether we see
ourselves as beautiful, or ugly, or desirable, or repulsive in
a sexual way. This picture is an idealized notion of what we
should be like: how we should look, how we should move,
how much at ease we should be in walking in front of a
group, and so on. Discomfort with one's body—or one
aspect of one's body—is often translated into blackest dis-
harmony with one's "self." Our self-esteem depends on our
body; our "self" is tied to our looks.

This self is a frail and vulnerable entity. It wants to feel
good at all costs. It looks for constant reassurance: inside,
one feels beautiful; outside, one needs improvement.
Whenever the self feels threatened and insecure, it will
resort to body affirmation. New clothes, fashionable shoes,

cosmetics, a favorite sport—even a house, an art collection, a hobby, or a motorcycle—can become a means of pleasing and reassuring the self by highlighting the body and its properties. We are forever trying to make our looks conform to our inner mental picture of ourselves—this "me" as we would *like* it to be.

Our self as expressed by our looks becomes paramount during adolescence. As babies we did not have a distinctive inner self. An infant is believed to think that his mother's breast is an extension of himself, and so is the rattle he holds in his hands. His world, according to one pioneer psychologist, is "one blooming, buzzing confusion." In time, he comes to see himself as a separate entity from his world. He learns to see himself as distinct from his body, and his body as distinct from the rest of the universe. During adolescence, the self is thought to be emerging; one's growing-up years are believed to be the period when separation of self and body occurs. Maturity is sometimes defined as the point where this process is completed, although a total separation of self and body may never quite take place.

It can easily be seen how this emerging self is taxed and burdened during one's growing-up years. Teen-agers frequently define and reject themselves in terms of their physical features or faults. Adolescents are notorious for their body clumsiness; at least they often feel as if they were "all arms and legs." They tend to think of their awkward, lanky bodies as the final edition of themselves—a painful stage for the self to live through:

> "I felt like a giraffe whenever I walked into my classroom. I was the tallest girl in the crowd—I stood a head taller than anyone else in my school. I was sure that any

sneer or smirk or giggle was meant to reduce me to dust. By the time I was thirteen I was as tall as I am now. . . . I came close to suicide, and I'm not kidding."

"As long as I can remember, I was handicapped by poor vision. I went through school taking low grades because I was too embarrassed to admit the world looked like one great big blur. Once my mother took me to an eye specialist to have me fitted for glasses. I took one horrified look at myself in the mirror and decided I'd rather flunk the class than wear those spectacles on my nose. I was in love with Linda at that time. . . . I was sure glasses would ruin any slim chances I might otherwise have."

A message coming our way that tells us we are less than attractive can be very disturbing and upsetting to our feeling of self-worth. A snapshot, we are sure, did not "catch us at our best." Mirrors, we feel, lie and distort. One's pallor is due to unfortunate lighting. Even one's name may feel funny and strange at times, as if it is not an adequate label to describe the more beautiful inner "me." We see ourselves with something like an inner eye against which the outer self—the body—is constantly compared and usually found lacking.

A good self-image is essential to inner balance and to good mental health. Therefore the body becomes a vehicle to serve this inner need: a fashionable dress, for example, or a classy pullover can do wonders for one's self-esteem. It is like a compliment we pay to ourselves: "I am beautiful," "I am desirable," "I feel lovely." A new hairstyle may be an attempt to say: "My inner self is unhappy with the way I look. I need to look better in order to feel better. I am going to change my looks so that my outer appearance more closely matches my inner feeling of being glamorous."

One's body features therefore become an extremely important means of building and preserving one's inner feeling of self-worth. There must be many girls who let the shape of their noses on one hand dictate self-esteem on the other. The wrong tilt of a girl's nose can become endowed with remarkably destructive properties: it influences how she believes boys evaluate her, how they treat her as a person, why they are mean or loving or attentive or ignoring, and so on. Similarly, a boy may be convinced that his oversized ears are to blame for his lack of rapport with desirable girls. A boy's flappy ears may be a painful embarrassment indeed, although oversized ears have never hurt a girl, while oversized feet may well have, at least on the dance floor. Strangely enough, self-evaluation appears to be more closely tied to the face and torso than to the extremities. Large and unbeautiful hands will rarely worry a girl, but a mouth just a shade too large or too small may make her growing-up years one never-ending stretch of misery.

Why is it that one's self selects a relatively minor aspect of one's body and magnifies it out of all proportion so that it receives the power to put a negative stamp on the whole personality? We do not know. But it seems evident that so strongly is our self-worth tied to our looks that harmony or agony with our facial symmetry or body shortcomings translates itself into harmony or displeasure with our whole being. So it becomes much harder to come to terms with limitations in one's looks than it is to admit to flaws in intelligence or personality. Our body image is tremendously emotionally loaded.

It can easily be understood, then, how loving someone sexually means being on vulnerable psychological grounds.

One's very essence seems at stake. If one's body is worth loving—if one's lips are pleasant to be kissed and one's body is worth being stroked, is that not a very powerful affirmation of one's self-worth? If a girl trembles when a boy kisses her, does that not mean that their bodies are beautiful and pleasing, and that therefore their selves are worth loving and caring? On a superficial level, sex would seem to be the perfect and logical remedy to help firm up one's self-esteem and feeling of self-worth.

The need to be loved in a physical way seems compelling, according to present psychological evidence. There are only two needs believed to be stronger: the need to have shelter, and the need to have food. Experiments with monkeys have shown that these animals, when deprived of physical touch while maturing, will be "abnormal" when fully grown in that they will not know how to care for their young, how to be loving and kind and unselfish. Other experiments with pets have shown over and over that physical fondling, stroking, and petting will produce more well-balanced, "happy," cooperative creatures than just giving food without "love." This seems to be true of humans as well: the more bodily love a young child receives, the greater a chance he has to turn out a well-balanced, happy, considerate, loving adult.

Babies may literally be "starved to death" by lack of physical love. Several years ago a documentary film was made that showed the tragic effects of the lack of adequate loving. It told the story of some ninety children, living in a South American orphanage, being cared for by nurses who provided the necessary comfort and food but were too understaffed and overworked to give these babies physical affection. There was no time for loving, stroking, rocking, kissing, and fondling. The babies were well fed, diapered when necessary, kept warm and comfortable, but otherwise left alone.

One third of these children were dead before the year was over. Before they died, they lost appetite, would cry for hours, their bodies would shrink, their faces would become empty and expressionless. Several more died the following year. Those who survived carried away for life deep, permanent emotional scars.

During infancy, most American children receive a good deal of touching and loving in a physical way, but this will drastically change as soon as school years begin—for little boys, earlier than that. A mother may refrain from kissing and fondling a boy for fear of making him "less of a man." A father may even be more fearful. A "manly" handshake may be all the physical touch that is given: "Who wants a sissy for a son?" Right after infancy, there is a decade or so of very little bodily loving. One can only speculate as to how terribly hungry some kids must be for intimate physical touch.

Then comes adolescence: young people fall in love. Making love is like a literal step back into infancy. Lovers rock and cuddle each other. They speak to each other in whispered, childish, teasing words. Often they even call each other "baby." It is a very weird experience, unlike anything felt since earliest childhood on. It does feel very good, and it is hard to stop!

But here's where our "self" comes in.

By now it has become a precious entity which has, after all, taken us a lifetime to build and construct. To protect our emotional investment, we have built emotional fences around the inner "me." These fences—boundaries around our inner self—have to do with physical nearness or distance.

In everyday life we show tremendous respect for these boundaries. We dress up far more for strangers than for friends, as if our self needs these additional barriers for protection. We mutter "Excuse me" when we pass another person, as if the briefest body nearness is an affront. We apologize profoundly when bumping into each other. Some people suffer acutely having to wait in line, or having to eat in a crowded restaurant, or being locked in an elevator with persons they might have to touch accidentally. We don't like people "rubbing us the wrong way." We become "touchy" if someone comes too near to our inner self. Even improper eye contact is avoided as if eyes could touch as well as hands. We think of staring as being very rude.

Flirting behavior is meant to test these physical and psychological boundaries. Flirting is a real approach-avoid affair. We strictly see to it that no one may overstep these boundaries against our will. At first, eyes will meet ever so briefly, and then quickly look away. Flirting is characterized by teasing, laughing, easy chatter, and provocative but covert body movements. It is almost painful to have eye contact with a person we scarcely know without superficial words to set the proper frame of reference. Glances may be "felt" as very unpleasant if touch is not yet wanted. As we come to know the other person better—as we are permitted to come nearer to the person's inner self—touching comes to be more tolerable with time.

It seems that emotional boundaries cannot be broken down at will without some inner cost to one's self. So-called encounter groups—meetings in which people try to break down boundaries for the sake of communication—are often charged with violating an inner principle by forcing people to "come out of their shells" before there is psychological readiness. Sometimes, during such meetings called "marathons," nudity is used as a means of speeding up the process of harmony between body and self. Many people find encounter groups of this sort extremely difficult to bear, charging that they force a false intimacy which ignores the inner currents that have to feel just right for two people to come to know each other on an intimate physical basis.

Boundaries around our self are gradually broken down by touching. Sometimes we say we are "touched" by an experience that moves us very deeply. "Keep in touch," we may say to a person we casually like, without, of course, expecting literal touch. Acquaintances will shake hands when parting. Friends will embrace. Lovers will kiss. Intercourse is the ultimate intimacy that two people may experience. The closer we are to another person, the better we will feel about touching and being touched.

As boundaries are gradually broken down, emotional bonds may be formed. Attraction between two people may be strengthened by touching. However, by no means will physical nearness per se always result in a strengthening of an emotional bond. Electrical impulses, which, after all, should be neutral, translate touch as pleasant if the person touching us is one with whom we have sufficient psychological nearness that touch can be tolerated. Being touched without willingness to be touched can be extremely difficult to bear. Sex without inner nearness may turn very ugly and unbearable if there is touching across the fence, so to speak. Few people can disguise how they feel about themselves and their bodies after consummated sex. Intercourse is more than a shedding of one's clothes; it is a psychological exposure that may evoke strong feelings of self-hate and disgust.

> "I had said 'no' to Rick all summer long . . . wanting to preserve that special feeling that was supposed to come with first sex. But all evening he made eyes at Rhonda, avoiding looking at me. I knew all too well what was on his mind. I struggled with myself. . . . Even when he took me home and I asked him in, I didn't want it to happen. My folks were in the other room; they could have come in at any moment. I hated to give in like that, but his hands were on my legs. . . . I couldn't stop him, but I hated it, I hated it all. I didn't like to do it in a hurry, with no feeling on either one's part, just as something that had to be done because there was by then no way *not* to do it."

In this case, intercourse was taking place on unprepared psychological grounds. There was an inner unwillingness to be invaded, and therefore touch was experienced as unpleasant and repulsive. This girl, in a way, was caught "between the devil and the deep blue sea"—her self-esteem was threatened by another girl, and she needed bodily affirmation telling her that she was lovable and wanted. But her experience was a bitter disappointment, nevertheless.

> "This was supposed to be the greatest, and it felt bad and wicked. It was supposed to feel good, and it was painful. It was supposed to bind us to each other, but when it was over, we were too ashamed to look into each other's faces. I've never felt more cheated in my life."

Each of us is an individually constructed psychological self, with unique individual emotional needs: needs for reassurance, needs for inner closeness, for feeling lovely and lovable, for feeling worthwhile as a self. We know—or maybe others who know have told us—that sex feels good in a very down-to-earth bodily way. Falling in love means tying a very special bond with a very special person who will, we hope, fulfill our emotional needs. There are inner compelling pushes that are very urgent and work in favor of sex. It is tempting to reach out and take one's warmth from whatever source is available and willing. But sex has to come according to an emotional prescription. Unless it truly feels tailor-made, there might well be those hidden fences and boundaries to interfere and make it ugly and cheap.

It would seem that the shock of such an experience could be devastating. Rarely, if ever, was there opportunity to learn beforehand the sheer physical sensations involved in being locked that intimately to a member of the opposite sex. Not since earliest childhood on have we permitted anyone to be that close. Intercourse taking place too soon, with the wrong partner, at the wrong time, under the wrong circumstances would seem to be a gross violation of the carefully protected inner self. Something like psychological rape may take place; it can be very painful emotionally to merge oneself with another person on such intimate psychological terrain.

This, perhaps, is a question that one might ask when considering premarital sex: Is it worth the psychological risk? How much nearness and intimacy can be borne by the self in a certain relationship? There may be some people who feel perfectly comfortable with easy, casual, noncommittal sex; most people, however, will not. The very fact that it is a furtive, hasty, hidden experience, taking place on the back seat of a car, to be experienced with an eye and an ear to discovery, makes premarital sex a very risky psycho-logical venture. Physical sex without emotional readiness would seem to be a violation of the inner self. Rarely is premarital sex of such nature that full intimacy can be experienced without at least some cost to one's self-esteem.

5

THE DEVIL'S TRIDENT

Guilt in a Cultural Setting

Most children, at a very early age, learn not to touch or even look at certain parts of their own or other people's bodies. As a rule, they never see their parents naked; seldom their brothers and sisters of the opposite sex. They are hushed into silence when they want to speak about their sexual organs and the sensations they experience when touching them. Ever since they were little, they were taught that a nude picture was a "dirty" picture, that their genitals were to be kept covered, that certain things were never talked about. Much of the sexual information they received came to them by way of the smutty joke, told by other children who knew no more than they but who had seen the smirk that went with it and who took pains to pass it on. Rather than learning to feel pride in what their bodies represent, many children thus learn that there is something mysteriously wrong with certain body parts. And in no time at all they come to weigh—before they dare to ask a curious question—whether it is a "good" or "wicked" kind of body knowledge that they seek.

This is how guilt gets hooked onto sex.

Young boys and girls discovering for the first time the pleasurable sensations located in the genital area will as a rule be burdened with a tremendous load of guilt. They cannot help having feelings about what they have done, and seldom will they think these feelings strong and good. They will keep their secret to themselves, terror-stricken, lest anyone find out. They begin to associate shame and guilt and fear with anything that resembles sex. This guilt, never talked about and never really understood, may become so painful that the child will force it underground, hoping it will bother him no more. But guilt repressed into the un-conscious will cause anxiety, and anxiety will undermine his self-esteem, because he finds it painful to live with himself as one who has used his body for something of which others —if they *knew*—would surely disapprove.

Restrictions placed on certain thoughts or deeds, seen as so terrible that often they don't even have a name, are called cultural taboos. A taboo stands for a "Hands off!" attitude, with heavy emotional penalties for those who don't obey.

Perhaps with the exception of taboos connected with religion, there are more taboos surrounding sex than can be found in any other area of life. This is strange in the sense that sexual behavior is the reason for our very existence and should therefore have a tremendously important place in our intellectual curiosity. It seems a paradox to deny sexual education its priority in our formal or informal education. Yet would any parent dream of actually teaching his child about sex by letting him watch intercourse? Unless we open the bedroom door by accident, we never see our parents making love, and chances are we will make very sure our children won't see us either.

Not all sexual taboos, however, have been "created equal," by any means. Some taboos travel lightly and are accepted almost with a shrug. The human navel, for example, has been in certain times and places tabooed, though it is hard to imagine a part of one's anatomy more harmless and nonthreatening. A girl's virginity is protected by social taboos, but they are conditional in that they can be broken and sanctioned with the proper wedding bells or in the name of love. Incest, however, is a taboo so repulsive and frightening to our ways of thinking that not even to ourselves will we admit to a sexual attraction to a member of our close family. Yet intellectually, incest would seem to be a natural outcome of close family living, since a great deal of loving and caring and touching goes on between brother and sister, or parent and child, or uncle and niece. Incest is one of the most threatening taboos we have invented; we would feel surely depraved if even a flicker of incestual desire would cross our thoughts.

Just as a child builds his self through information from his body, he *evaluates* this self through feedback from his culture. Starting with the third year of life, a child begins to evaluate his behavior by the smiles and the frowns of other people. A small child identifies "good" with comfort and "bad" with blocked desires. Children don't just eat; there's praise for eating the right kind of food, in the right amount, at the right time, according to a certain ritual and certain rules laid down by important and powerful people. One can't just suck the gravy off one's fingers, even though no real harm would come to oneself or others if one did. Parents hover over an infant's chair with their strength and their power and their know-how—they are pretty convincing if one is little and they are big! Smiles are rewards for "right" behavior, frowns or a slap on one's backside for "bad." Someone bigger and stronger than the child dictates the shape and direction of his wishes and what he does to see to it that they are satisfied.

As the young child makes his first exploratory steps into the neighborhood, there are others who tell him right from wrong. His life is shared with other people who have definite convictions about those things he can or cannot do. He learns, for example, that a certain kind of curiosity on his part may backfire and hurt his social chances very badly.

> "I was six at the time; Susie must have been about four. We were just fooling around. . . . This was in our basement, behind the fruit jars. We both thought our discoveries hilarious but knew enough to keep a straight face in front of Mom. We had several repeats, I remember, until we were finally caught. I've never seen my mom so angry. Of course I got a licking, but that was not the end of it by any means. Somehow word got around. I became the outcast of the entire neighborhood. I don't think I was invited to a single birthday party after that."

Such learning is powerful learning indeed. It is difficult, even impossible at times, to unlearn what we have learned so thoroughly in our most impressionable years.

A young person has no way of knowing on his own what his behavior in culture is to be. Therefore he takes the cultural blueprint as his measuring rod. In a way, he uses culture like a mirror: Do I still look all right if I do this, or if I want that? Will I be loved, or will I be hurt? The self he will develop will depend in part on the kinds of persons he will meet, and the kinds of beliefs these persons hold. Personalities are built through being involved in very many intimate or casual relationships. More often than not, sexual attitudes, forming a part of one's self, come early to be associated with many moral terrors because learning along the way was shaped and directed by someone important who disapproved.

Many people in time become convinced that they just *know,* deep down in their hearts, when certain things concerning sex are wrong. Often it is believed that conscience is the direct voice of God—that whatever one's conscience forbids must be wrong and whatever one's conscience okays must be all right. But no clergyman or priest or rabbi would advise us to trust our conscience completely in everything. Our conscience is not a totally reliable compass to guide us in what is right and what is wrong, for it has been educated and taught by other people, and reflects what *they* believe is right or wrong. Some people believe that it is wrong to eat beef and others don't give that a second thought. Some people are convinced that it is wrong to shave and to wear buttons on one's shirt, and others think such beliefs are ridiculous. Most people think that it is wrong to steal, but some would say that under certain circumstances stealing could be condoned, such as a mother stealing food for her hungry child. The same thing can be said about murder, and dancing, and marihuana, and wearing miniskirts, and flattering people, and premarital sex. The conscience could not be the undiluted voice of God or it would not tell an Amishman to keep his beard and a sophisticated New Yorker to shave it off each morning. Conscience is heavily influenced by what others tell us during a time when we are still too young to make up our minds for ourselves, and what others have told us may be very wrong as still other people see things. Our conscience, in our early years, is a very malleable thing.

An indication of how powerful a dictator our conscience can become can be seen by the guilt associated with masturbation. It is a matter of scientific fact that physically there is no harm in masturbation. It does not "cause" anything—not insanity nor dizziness nor a wart on one's nose. Most professionals agree that masturbation is a harmless source of pleasure and a valuable tension relief vent. Some are even beginning to advocate that it should be taught to the young as a legitimate means of finding some bodily comfort during times when sexual urges are strongest and intercourse is still taboo.

But society is squeamish about masturbation. Its practice is very much a cultural taboo. There are no hints regarding the joys of masturbation along highway billboards, although there are very many variations about heterosexual love. Advertisers know better than to promote their products via masturbation themes, though they probably would if it were an acceptable avenue for sex. Texts don't usually mention it; if advice is given at all, it is to the effect that masturbation should be practiced behind locked bathroom doors, and the less said about it, the better! One doesn't talk comfortably about things done behind locked bathroom doors, even to one's friends. It is an easy step from there to associate masturbation with being "unclean" and to feel guilty for doing a "dirty" thing with one's body.

Girls, especially, build certain feelings of being "unclean" around their normal body functions. Menstruation is a taboo in very many societies, including to a degree our

own society. Advertisers promoting products of feminine
hygiene often claim that their products will help girls "feel
as if they were normal." This sales pitch is even whispered
in several television ads. In addition, bleeding is usually
associated with damage and with injury; many women,
therefore, will speak of menstruating as "having the curse"
or, more mysteriously and guiltily, as having "one of those
days." Similarly, after the birth of a baby, a woman's breasts
will swell with milk. Doctors tell us that nursing is one of
the cleanest, healthiest, and most satisfying experiences that
can happen to a baby. However, if lactation and nursing are
seen as body functions to be hidden, it is easy to associate
such changes with animals, especially cows. And how many
nursing mothers *do* we see?

It is often claimed that taboos are useful because they
make for an orderly, civilized life. But taboos have a way
of hanging around in a culture long after their usefulness
has expired. Taboos have a way of living on through many
centuries, and even though necessary at one time, they may
no longer make sense today. For example, during the times
of the great Crusades, hopeless, nonsexual love was thought
to be the best way to live and to love to the fullest. Therefore, guilty knights and romantic damsels slept together
without touching each other in order to "purify" their love.
As a protection against temptation, they sometimes even
kept a drawn sword between them as a reminder. The legend of Tristan and Isolde describes such "perfect" nonsexual love. More than a thousand years afterward, our Western culture still shows traces of this belief. Catholic nuns and
monks still choose celibacy as a means of "purifying" their
love for all mankind, and the Catholic Church still resists
doing away with this cherished belief, even though many

young men and women belonging to the Catholic Church feel strongly that such beliefs have no place in today's modern world.

Even in everyday life, we often believe that by ignoring the sexual appetite, a higher form of love can be achieved. Often, it is stipulated that a woman should be very difficult to possess, otherwise she cannot be regarded as precious. A prostitute is "cheap," regardless of what she may charge, because she is available. A girl too generous with her sexual favors loses her value in boys' eyes very rapidly, too. It seems almost noble to suffer for desires that cannot be fulfilled. Virtue, seen in this light, becomes synonymous with prudishness.

Many people complain that our culture has inherited more than its share of sexual taboos. Time and again Western man has turned against his body and his sexuality. Many peoples of the world have consistently equated sex with evil and with darkness. Sex has always been viewed as something that had to be hidden, to be practiced in darkness, behind locked doors, in secrecy and with furtiveness. Our sexual attitudes are a product of our world; we have learned them from our parents, teachers, friends, enemies, the mass media, and the church. There are many shocking and lasting lessons along the way to adulthood that sex is quite offensive and that therefore, if practiced, it should at least be kept out of sight. It is a message that we have heard so many times that it is impossible to ignore what has seeped into our very pores.

There is a price tag to cultural taboos. Those individuals who have been brought up with strong sexual prohibitions never really learn to feel decently about sex even within marriage or they wouldn't be so secretive with their own

children in return. Many people have difficulty having their
bodies examined in a doctor's office without a strong feeling
of "wrongness." Physicians will testify to the fact that it is
agony for many women to speak about sexual matters per-
taining to their married lives. Men may talk to other men,
but often in derogatory fashion: in crude jokes or facetious
quips, belittling themselves and their actions and verbally
degrading their partners. It was not very long ago that
women were not supposed to have—and were not believed
to have—any sexual desires at all. Even our scientists, until
very recently, averted their curiosity from investigating the
factors involved in human sexuality. There is, for example,
not yet an adequate description of the clitoris, that area
within a woman's genitals which is most sensitive to stimulation.

Many of us have learned to react as if every time we
touch sex, our conscience gives us some kind of shock. So
the best way to avoid pain is not to touch sex, or to touch
it only in a noncommittal manner. The values of the culture
are thus internalized by means of psychological blackmail,
so to speak. Guilt, like love, comes to be a man-made creation. With love, our inner needs and expectations decide
how we feel. With guilt, our culture has decided for us what
we *should* feel. Guilt is a means of making us see our experiences in a certain light, compared and evaluated against a
cultural norm.

A message repeated over and over takes on a life of its
own. It becomes very meaningful in time, often against our
will. If everyone is doing the same thing—be it wearing a
smile button or racing tennis shoes or going bra-less or
abstaining from premarital sex—it's easier to go along, and
it's difficult to go against the tide. Who wants to be a sore

thumb? It hurts to step into forbidden territory. There are
emotional hazards in going against the majority opinion;
above all, there is painful rejection. Even a seagull named
Jonathan learned that to his dismay.

Cultural values, therefore, come to be invested with a
great deal of personal emotion. There is comfort in going
along with the crowd, and there are costs in *not* doing so:
costs in status, or inner peace, or feeling of safety, or belonging. And in no time at all it is not our belief that is on trial
but *us*. It is not masturbation per se which is so terrible but
what we think of ourselves as a result. It hurts our self to violate
a principle that we personally have come to hold very dear.
In Freudian thinking, we have learned to invest more and
more in the superego and less and less in the id. We have
come to value inner controls. We have come to see that
there are psychological benefits in bringing our actions into
harmony with our beliefs. Life can be unpleasant if conscience is at odds with what we do. It is almost as if conscience, standing there in place of parents, spanked the
"child" for doing the forbidden deed.

Guilt thus becomes the alarm bell that warns us when we
have strayed from the prescribed cultural path. Guilt is the
reaction to having overstepped some boundaries, to having
violated a moral code, to having broken through a prohibi-
tion. And guilt cannot easily be ignored. Guilt has many
ways of making its presence known. The body may react
because the self feels threatened. It may be a vague uneasi-
ness that is felt in the pit of one's stomach, or it may be an
all-pervasive horrible feeling of having one's whole personality "poisoned" by wrongness in thought or deed. Guilt,
we feel, is literally "written in our face" when we blush.
Folklore has it that blushing is nature's attempt to conceal.

Lowered eyelashes, hunched shoulders, covered lips—all these are attempts at concealment. Often, guilty people try to hide their hands as well. Orientals speak of "losing face" when feeling guilty or shamed. Even Adam and Eve took cover behind the proverbial fig leaf because of guilt.

A guilty person will almost always try to cover up, often by psychological means:

Some girls prefer to have sexual relations only in the dark, where their bodies cannot be seen, or prefer to keep some clothing on. It is a means of holding on to some of the restraints. Other girls try to avoid guilt by being as uninvolved emotionally as they could possibly be. They put all the blame for sexual desires on their partners: "He wants it and I do it only because he insists." Still others find it much easier to have intercourse than to talk about it. Some handle their feelings of guilt by laughing and joking about sex, as if by making light of sex the danger to one's self can be minimized. Some girls will use the "All but . . ." technique, telling themselves that sex is not sex unless it's intercourse. Still others are content to do their forbidden deeds in secrecy, happy in the knowledge that they are breaking some sacred rule:

> "When our pastor—whom I had never liked—put his hands on my veil and blessed our union, I felt a wild surge of triumph. Ours was a small community, and rules and expectations regarding virginity were very strict. I knew of no girl who had had sex before marriage, but I had tried it and I was proud that I did not let our pastor tell me what to do."

One couple even tried to bribe conscience:

> "My mom had made a strict rule: whenever Craig would
> visit, we were to leave the door open a 'book's width.' We
> obeyed scrupulously. . . . Every time we went to bed to-
> gether, we stuck a matchbook between jamb and door."

Still more hidden ways of dealing with guilt may be
constant apologizing, or suppressing sexual wishes, or looking for excuses, or paying for the "damage" done, or com-
pensating by taking all the blame.

It would be good if all of us could agree on what is right
and what is wrong, so that we knew exactly when to feel
guilty and in what proportion. Guilt has its place as a cultural safeguard and helps us feel some inner decency. It just
seems that sex demands a lion's share of guilt. Teen-agers
can come to feel very guilty for things that may deserve only
a little guilt. A girl can come to believe that she is very
wicked for holding her boy friend's hand if her parents have
taught her that premarital handholding is wrong. A boy may
feel wretched for having had sexual dreams, but will not bat
an eyelash about having cheated in an exam, or having
tricked a girl, or having double-crossed a friend.

6

NOTCHES ON BEDPOSTS

The Masculine Image

Several years ago a number of men in Hong Kong complained about a very strange malady. They were "shrinking" where it mattered most, they told their doctors in alarm. Could a man's organ, they asked fearfully, simply disappear into his lower abdomen? As a precaution, some had tied a string around their precious possession so as to be able to pull it out again. Others kept one hand in their pocket at all times, afraid to let go. Still others avoided intercourse or even cold baths, since they had observed that such activity diminished the size of their genitals.

Psychotherapy revealed that this fear, though silly and irrational, was based on their worry of failing sexually, of being unable to perform during intercourse. A penis, to a male, has always been an extremely valuable thing, and its loss—or the loss of its function—a stark and threatening reality. Many psychotherapists believe that the fear of being castrated is part of every man's psyche, whether he consciously knows it or not.

Rituals surrounding the phallus and its size were probably among the first religious rites practiced by prehistoric man. Never have women's genitals been seen as nearly that important. In fact, some tribes practiced rituals during which a girl's clitoris was surgically removed in order to decrease her capacity for passion and thereby increase her price on the marriage market. A girl thus "treated" would keep her virginity and therefore be more valuable to a male. In contrast, a man's capacity for passion—his virility—was seen as his greatest asset, to be protected against witches and sorcerers who plotted to come and steal it by night. Since it had been observed that castration made animals less spirited creatures, surgery was often used to humiliate the male enemy by cutting away his masculinity without taking away his life.

An adolescent boy in our days will usually think of his penis as something important, but something that is taken for granted and matter-of-fact. A penis is a visible and concrete thing, an organ to be *used,* and by no means for pleasure alone.

It serves double plumbing, so to speak. It transmits the urine from the bladder as well as the semen from the testicles and glands. A boy has his equipment handy. It is located on the outside of his body; he is free to touch it and examine it and marvel at its excitable properties. He handles his penis casually every day. He may be proud of its size; it looks like a bold and obvious symbol of being a male. It is not hidden and secretive, like a girl's clitoris which serves no other function than to give her pleasure in sex.

This chapter and the next will deal with some of the

psychological reasons why boys seem to take to sex so much
more casually than girls. Boys find it difficult to understand
why girls need a great deal of handholding and kissing and
being told that they are lovable and loved before they really
warm up to the idea of wanting intercourse. Boys are more
like gasoline, ready to ignite with any match. Sexual arousal
comes quickly to a male. It can—and often does—make him
impatient, clumsy, hurried, and brutal, and he may forget
how important a gradual approach can be. Females, typically, need a lot of patient kindling before their limbs finally
catch fire, although eventually they burn with just as passionate a heat. A boy will often find it difficult to understand
why a girl doesn't seem to be as "quick on the trigger" as
he is. On the other hand, many girls find it difficult to
sympathize with the strength of a boy's desire and the ur-
gency of sexual pressure on a male. Some men are convinced that a woman should permit intercourse at any time
and under any circumstances, since physically she is always
"ready," while a man is at the mercy of his erectile powers.
Often the conflict is explained by these anatomical differences in arousability. It is taken for granted that nature has
somehow given males and females different miles per hour
gauges on which to judge their speed in wanting sex.

We will, instead, speculate a little about other reasons
that may have a say in attitudes surrounding sex. Boys are
often accused of impersonality in sex. They seem to be
satisfied just looking at a body without feeling the need to
get acquainted with the person inside that sexy shell. A
breast is a breast, and a thigh is a thigh, whether it belongs
to Jane Brown or Letticia Thurbingowe. The body parts are
interchangeable, like the parts in a Ford engine.

Many girls, in contrast, view sex as something of the

nature of a secret luxury, to be used sparingly and with discrimination. Girls take their femininity on faith, as something they expect to grow into as soon as they grow up. A girl is not as preoccupied with sexual equipment the way this is true of a boy. Chances are a girl does not even know the terms for some of her anatomical parts, such as the clitoris. She may have discovered its presence by accident and never told anyone about her discovery. Somewhere along the way she may have been told that inside her body there are two tiny, treelike organs that serve to prepare her for motherhood, but she has to *believe* this: she has no way of looking at her ovaries and coming to grasp their reality. A boy can touch his penis and feel the testicles inside the scrotum and wonder in a far more concrete way just what it takes that will make of him a man.

> "Well, you know, I am kind of short. In the shower I noticed that my penis was just a little peanut. I told a doctor about my fears, but he just laughed and said there were two kinds, the kind that hung down until excited and then stood up, and the kind that was little until excited and then grew longer, and that both were just as long and good. That made me feel a little better. But I'll never forget how relieved I was when a bunch of us in high school got to use microscopes in the lab. After school when no one was around, each of us took some of his sperm and looked at it under the microscope. I felt so glad and relieved when I saw that mine had things in it that wiggled. I knew I was really a man."

In our culture, men are seen as the ones who call the shots. Men see to it that things get *done,* and done *efficiently.* Men actively penetrate; women passively "permit" penetration. A man's sperm wiggles up to the Fallopian tubes; a woman's egg "just sits and waits." Man can "finish" his important work for procreation in a matter of minutes, leaving the woman helplessly "stuck" with a baby for many years to come. Hairy-chested magazines promote the image of *man the doer*—active in the outdoors, discovering the wilderness, conquering and ruling the world, by force and ruthlessness if necessary. On the screen, the Western hero displaying a powerful gun is a perennial Hollywood box office attraction. Males, even in the animal world, are usually stronger, louder, bolder. Boys speak louder and have a more forceful stride than do girls. Just as a peacock spreads his feathers to impress his private chickenworld, men often try to spread an image of themselves as physical and virile and visible in an unmistakable way.

A man in our society is always conscious of the role he has to play. He is an actor on the stage. Performance comes to matter terribly. And it is sexual performance that many see as *the* performance which makes out of a boy a man. Our culture sees sex as the great indoor sport where one is expected to play one's role with skill, ardor, and imagination; it follows, therefore, that one's status, one's feelings of self-worth, and one's image *depend on the way this role is carried out.*

Some people have asked the question why sexual performance—since it is such an all-important event—is therefore not taught to the young as a matter of routine. The answer given is usually that sex is something that should come naturally. Animals, after all, don't have to be taught, so why should boys and girls? We do not think of sex as something that requires special skill, although we do think that any other activity worth doing needs practice and can be improved by repetition. Naïvely we hope that first sex will be just great. Even though no one has told us or shown us how it is to be done, we somehow blissfully expect an automatic perfect "hit" the very first time around.

> "We hadn't planned it at all . . . but here we were doing it. . . . We couldn't stop! It wasn't even fun; the car was too small and her knees were in the way and she was as rigid as a board. Then I realized that her face was wet from tears and I was embarrassed to death and I knew I didn't care if I never saw her again. I've never felt more rotten in my life."

Just as our table manners need educating, our sexual behavior needs educating too. We need to be taught how to become coherently male or female. As it happens, we *are* taught—indirectly, perhaps, but very convincingly. Such learning comes to us by way of sexual *roles.*

The term "role" is ultimately derived from the Latin word *rotulus,* denoting a little wheel. The spokes of a wheel turn in an orderly way; a role is an orderly model of behavior. Playing the male or female role means having sex according to a cultural script.

Society hands boys and girls a different script as to what their sexual lines are to be—how they are to function in their sexual capacity. And no role division could be harsher. There is probably not yet a culture in this world which treats its males and females equally alike. There are different rules, different norms, different expectations. For better or worse, "correct behavior" often means "correct sex behavior": "Do you perform the way a man ought to perform?" "Do you react the way a woman should?" The social cues coming our way give us our sexual direction. We live in our world as male and female, boys and girls, men and women. The way we are treated by others, our emotional reactions, the attitudes and opinions we will hold, the jobs we will choose, are largely determined by the fact of our respective sex.

These cues have been fed to us since very early infancy. Only for a very short time in our embryonic life—for about six weeks from the time of conception on—did it look as if we could have developed as either male or female. But from the day a mother wraps her newborn baby in either pink or blue, this child will experience the world in relation to his or her respective sex. Studies have shown that girls are handled much more gently than are boys. Boys are *expected* to be more active, to break their toys, to yell, to be demanding, to assert themselves in such a way that attention is being paid to who they are and what they do. Males in the Western world are *action-oriented.*

As boys and girls grow up, they are sharply segregated in the way they learn their sexual image. If mingling occurs at all, it seems to be in one direction only. A girl is permitted to have a boy's name; a boy is deeply offended if his name is spelled "Jo" instead of "Joe." A girl may wear slacks; a boy wouldn't be caught dead wearing a skirt or a dress. It's cute to be a tomboy; it's a social disgrace indeed to be called a girl or a sissy. A boy learns very early that his maleness is held in high esteem. He realizes that there is an image to be maintained. Often, this need to maintain an image may cause a boy to feel contempt for a girl who is seen as a giggling, foolish, frivolous creature—nothing but a nuisance to be brushed aside as compared to the importance attached to being a male.

As a boy learns his sexual image, he comes to hang on to that image of maleness with all his might. Our society sets stringent rules about the way a man and a woman are to behave, even in bed. It is "proper" for the male to be the sexual aggressor, and for the female to respond in an aloof, detached, and generally disinterested way.

The role becomes an attitude, a mental set. A boy's image of himself, his mental picture of how powerful he is, depends on how strong he feels his sexual prowess to be. If he is at all uncertain about himself and his maleness, it seems natural to turn to his penis and intercourse as a means for repeated reassurance.

The size of the penis and the frequency of sexual activity thus become extremely important in time. The penis takes on emotional significance, just like a badge that signifies proud membership in an exclusive club. Sigmund Freud, speculating on female sexuality, stated that in the depths of her heart every girl and woman was envious of the man, and felt cheated, betrayed, castrated, and furious for lacking the essential thing—an organ that symbolizes power and control. Later psychologists have modified this point of view. They say that "penis envy" does exist, but that men envy *each other*—it is not so much that female envies male.

Attaching such importance to the male organ is in a way ironic because a penis is by no means the thing that gives a man his masculinity. Internal biological and biochemical characteristics are responsible for the differences between the sexes. Male and female chromosomes are different. Male and female glands and secretions are different. The hormonal message carried in the bloodstream is very different in many ways. What we think of as the important sexual organs—the male penis and the female vagina—are actually nothing more than incidental signposts that advertise differently constructed biochemical building blocks of which male and female bodies are constructed.

Boys, much more than girls, have difficulty thinking of

their sexuality in this way, as something that is *given* to them by nature, repeated in every cell in their bodies, and therefore unalterable and all-pervasive and permanent. Boys think of masculinity as something to be *earned*.

The adolescent boy, for example, has heard and read for many years about the things men are supposed to accomplish sexually, and now he is becoming a man and knows that sooner or later he will have to do what normal boys and girls are supposed to do. Now the testing time is upon him. Will he be able to "make it"? Or will he fail?

> "I had argued with Linda for many weeks. She was a stubborn girl; she kept saying no. I kept saying: 'Why not, if you love me?' She said, 'I love you but I'm scared. . . .' I said I'd do it, all she had to do was to close her eyes and let me. Finally she gave in. . . . The bottom dropped out from under me. I was scared spitless, and I'm not kidding."

Intercourse puts a man to the test in a very concrete way. He feels he is expected to become an expert at a skill he has never had reason or chance to practice. He is not really sure about the role he is to play, but this he knows: he is a man, or *he had better be!* If one has doubts about one's sexual role, what better way to prove one's manliness than through intercourse? And it is ironic that many males feel they cannot have intercourse once and have it over with and done and put their doubts and fears to rest. Because a boy's penis is such an important source of self-esteem, he cannot bear to have it fail him even once. That is as good as an attack upon the self. A male may even feel that his reputation as a lover is only as good as his last performance—it is always open to challenge. Impotence, in a very concrete way, signals a serious threat. There's a hazard to his social self. His masculinity is not a "given"; it has to be earned by the sweat of his brow.

It is this fear of failure which largely accounts for the different attitudes that men and women attach to the matter of intercourse. An erection can be achieved in seconds by most men; typically, a man can be thinking about something completely different, have his attention turned to sex, have intercourse, and then lose interest in his partner—all in a very short span of time. Years ago a popular song went: "Give me five minutes more, only five minutes more. . . ." Some of the boys with their minds on sex revised it and sang: "Give me one minute more, I won't need the other four. . . ." Because sex can hold terror and failure, boys sometimes attack it in what seems to be an attitude of gritted teeth. Their erection is by no means an automatic thing that can always function on command. A male is very much on trial in the sexual situation because he can be short-circuited easily and suddenly. If he is worried and anxious about his potency, he creates a psychological set—a frame of reference for failure—that makes it difficult for him to be confident. Fear breeds fear, and failure failure. Worrying about one's sexual adequacy can be a most unnerving thing.

Some boys worry about whether they can make it by having an erection as soon as they want it to happen, or having it at the right time, or maintaining it long enough through intercourse, and the like. Some of them who make it a point to sound and act very sexy are really very fearful that their sexual powers might fail. Some men are so worried about being able to make it sexually that they would rather not have anything to do with sex at all because they don't like to be reminded of their inadequacy. A person will stay away from the ski slopes, too, who has never been any good at skiing. But the very act of avoiding the danger means that there is failure to be feared. A man who keeps conquering a long string of partners may have a need to prove to himself over and over that he is functioning all right. He is in need of constant validation.

This is why a boy learns early to advertise how good he is—or soon expects to be—in his powerful sexual role. Being able to display his virility—his sexiness—is a way of proving to himself and to others that he is "good," that he is confident and competent in sexual endeavors. Successfully carrying out the act of intercourse is a way of proving to himself, his sexual partner, and the world that he is certainly all right in areas where it counts. And learning being what it seems to be—that is, an increase of behavior associated with pleasure—sex becomes largely a *mentally cultivated habit.* The appetite grows by what it feeds on. The number of girls laid become notches on a boy's bedpost. The number of hearts broken are a boost to his ego. Girls come to be laid assembly-line fashion, with no criteria other than a minimum passing grade. Some high school boys keep lists of girls with whom they have had intercourse. They may compare rankings and notes as to "how many cherries a boy has to his credit." Being able to brag about sex with an air of sophistication gives them a feeling of experience and maturity and adequacy as men. Off-color jokes seem hilarious. Grubby sex in alleys seems O.K. It all serves a purpose. It helps the self to acquire a proud sexual role spelled "masculinity."

All this is to show why it is that males may bring certain uncaring attitudes to the sexual act; why some boys go after sex without a shred of feeling being exchanged. Manliness means virility and prowess and courage and even a certain cruelty. By talking flippantly and in an offhand manner about one's sexual conquests, by joking about sex, by looking at suggestive pictures, one earns great prestige for one's self. Taking a girl's virginity is something to brag about to one's friends; one's social ego feeds on such conquests.

Many boys thus come to see sex as their natural right, to be consumed by sole virtue of their being male. It stands in the way of perceiving their partners as persons with feelings and emotions of their own. For many a boy, a girl used in sex is an accessory. Whatever else love means in sex, it should mean relating to one's partner as a person and not as a convenient mechanical device. In selfish sex, a partner is seen as a fixture, to be used thoughtlessly and to be put out of sight after use. Of course there may be flirting and teasing and necking and whispered sweet lies, but these are seen as part of the "chase" or the "necessary price." Flattering a girl in order to get her to bed is little different, psychologically, from paying a prostitute in order to get her to strip.

The male, in many ways, is "caught" by his own sexual role. Because he is compelled to attach his masculinity to the function of his organ at any cost, he often cannot be genuine in lovemaking. Whatever he does sexually, he compares it mentally with what he *should* be like: there is a tremendous emotional investment in performance. Since much is at stake for the male, much can be lost.

No male is probably quite free from all fears that, if suddenly put to the test, he may fail to rise to the occasion, so to speak.

7

VALENTINE'S FLAVORS

The Feminine Counterpart

When it comes to having sex on the spur of the moment, a woman is far less hampered than a man. A woman can always pretend. Her anatomy is on her side: she needs no special readiness to be able to have intercourse. Physically, she is not prone to public humiliation. Yet women are more cautious and reluctant about casual sex.

This chapter will try to explain why men and women are plugged into different psychological circuits, why they seem to use their emotional capacities unequally. While a man might want to have sex—here, now, simple, direct, and physical—a woman will want to be loved and kissed and fussed over before she even feels like having intercourse. He wants sex if he thinks her pretty and likable; she needs frills and candlelight and whispered words of love. Often it is asserted that men and women have nothing in common *except* sex.

It looks as if nature has designated to the sexes a different psychological platform from which they operate. Men seem to have certain patterns of feelings and reactions, and women quite others. A man is expected to "rule" with his head; a woman is believed to "be ruled" by her heart. We think of "reason" as a masculine attribute; of "feeling" as belonging more to the feminine psyche. We assume an irrevocable split between male and female emotionality; if we see harmony between the sexes at all, it is in their respective *complementary* roles—like dancers on the dance floor, with one leading and the other being led. In simpler words, it looks as if women need more of this commodity called love.

Women, much more than men, like to have sex aesthetic and beautiful. "Does my hair look attractive?" "Can we have some soft music?" "Do you love me—forever and ever and ever?" Many men find this irritating; intercourse is intercourse, whether the floor has been swept during the past week or not. But for most women, beauty, privacy, and romance are very important, and even though the man may say he doesn't care for such nonsense, and may actually feel this way, the woman will still want to "feel right," for *her* sake. For a man, sex may fulfill a physical need; for a woman, it seems to satisfy a psychological need. In probing some of the reasons why a female has these greater emotional needs, we will assume that these needs *are* a reality, because they can be observed in everyday life, and they show up consistently on psychological measuring instruments called personality tests.

It would, of course, be possible to explain a woman's psychological makeup as a behavioral carbon copy of female sexual anatomy. It is possible to say that just as a man pat-

terns many of his personality characteristics on the characteristics of his penis and its function and therefore behaves
in a bold, outward, and thrusting way, a woman strives to
be mysterious and secretive and yielding because these are
the properties of her vagina. There are several theories, in
fact, which build on these hypotheses.

This chapter will take a different approach and give some
learned reasons why a female, on the receiving end of intercourse, brings certain emotional needs to the sexual act that
are different from the needs of the male—indeed, that are
often perceived to stand askew of his needs. The previous
chapter has already shown that when a society teaches its
young to be male and female, it teaches them in different
ways.

To most women, intercourse is by no means an act that
is hilarious and that lends itself to quips and jokes once it
is over. Sex, to a female, is a profound emotional commit-
ment. In order for her to find pleasure in sex, she needs to
be involved. She needs to love her partner, and she will
strive very hard to make him fall in love with her.

This need to love and be loved is in the foreground. It
is a profoundly compelling need; her sexual involvement
with a man will almost always be the by-product of a *prior*
emotional attachment. To a female, feelings come very
much first.

Much to the distress of many boys, girls therefore con-
sider love a prerequisite for sex. A girl usually does not wish
to be involved with sex unless she feels a psychological "fit"
with her partner. There simply is no meaning for her in sex
unless it is the outcome of a deeply stirring emotion. She
cannot understand why a male would want intercourse and
would not want *her*—how a man can act on a physical im-

pulse and dissociate himself from emotion and affection. Once the sex act is over, if love is lacking or superficial, a girl may feel depleted and drained and sex itself will become repugnant and will be associated with feelings of hatred and disgust. For a female, a sexual surrender is an emotional surrender, with all the vulnerability that such a step implies. To feel safe, to feel loved, in such a moment is a profound necessity. All too often a woman's first sexual experience is remembered with disgust, disillusionment, and sometimes even horror. "I felt as if I had been raped," is a common response.

Let's speculate a little on why this should be so.

A girl's emotions, for one, are not trained to respond to a sexual situation without having her deepest feelings involved in the act. In our society where girls are educated from earliest childhood on to have a horror of casual sex, the shock of the enchantment and wonder of sex can be devastating. Suddenly there is closeness, and this closeness can be unbearably sweet. Suddenly a boy and a girl hold hands, kiss, caress each other. A boy, in such a situation, is expected—even encouraged—to act in a ruthless fashion: to break down the barriers, to seduce, to conquer, to sweep the reluctant girl off her feet. He will test the sincerity of her reluctance with all the cunning at his command. He will accuse her bitterly of "not loving" him. The girl, who has been taught for many years that to give her body without feelings would be disloyal to her self, who has been taught that she would *never* want to kiss a boy unless she *really* loved him, will helplessly try to reconcile her clashing emotions while warding off the boy. She *wants* to kiss him; in fact, she too wants intercourse. It is easy for her to think that therefore the sensations she experiences *are* genuine love and to conclude that the person who arouses these feelings in her is the object of her love. In the silvery light of a full moon it is easy to confuse sex hunger with love, and to use "love" as a strategy to satisfy sex.

Another reason why love has priority over raw sexual feelings in a female is that sex, for its own sake, was very much discouraged in a woman until very recently. Girls had to be guarded and sheltered against the wickedness of men. For a long time, sex was seen as an act of obligation, almost a sacrifice. It could be "endured" only under the cloak of love. Not so long ago, a frigid woman was thought to be a virtuous woman. Women were not supposed to enjoy sex; it was something they put up with for the sake of a man's strange desires. A woman who had been raped was often questioned on whether she had enjoyed the experience, and was "forgiven" only if she could convince her fellow citizens that she did not. Even today, it is common to see surrender of virginity as an act of sacrifice—a terrible calamity to lose one's innocence without love!

This may be why frigidity in a woman—the equivalent of impotence in a man—is far less threatening to her. She is not nearly as concerned about a "power failure" the way this is true of her partner. Women rarely feel guilty about not being "turned on"; they are quick to claim that if the sparks are missing, it is simply because love is missing in the relationship.

Love and sex, in the eyes of most girls, are by no means the same ingredient in different wrappings.

"Well, he just paws me over a little and says: 'Let's have a party,' and I'm supposed to be as excited about it as he is."

"Sex, to Pete, is less romantic than a sneeze. It's there, you can't help it, you've got to let go. When it's over, it's over. . . . So what's the big deal? He can't understand how such an attitude offends my feelings."

Another reason why feelings of love are so important to a girl is that she has been permitted to show deep emotions before, while emotions may well have been taboo for a boy. A girl is permitted to be in touch with the currents of her emotional world much more than is a boy. A boy is taught to detest emotionality; boys *never* cry! A man will often feel a need to protect his inner feelings in a sexual involvement. His psychological comfort will demand that he tell himself —and his partner, for good measure—that he wants nothing but raw sex. A girl can't afford to be practical and nonemotional and nonclinging. If there's a touch of hardheadedness in her, it will be seen as being at the expense of her femininity.

Girls come to be sensitized to "love" in other ways as well. A man assesses his masculinity by his *own* responses; a woman assesses her femininity *by how others respond to her.* In the previous chapter, we saw that men get credit for what they do. Women get credit for what they *are,* personality-wise and beauty-wise. A man must prove his masculinity; a woman need only look seductive and tempting while waiting. Her sexual role is strengthened by the aesthetic properties of her body; it is not at all attached to the function of her body in sex. Her body is a means to an end—through her body, affection can be given or taken. Sex can be a way of saying: "How good-looking and lovable am I?" "Am I lovable enough that a boy would want to go to bed with me?" Or, "Am I just a second-rate goof-off whom nobody but second-rate people would want?" Seducing someone sexually is a way of reassurance that one is attractive and lovable and nice. Wanting to please, therefore, by "falling in love" becomes a political means. It is not at all in the emotional interest of a girl to have a string of lovers and thereby keep her involvement superficial and noncommittal. She is after emotional depth, which takes time and patience building up. She is more likely to place great emotional demands on one male than to spread herself thin over very many relationships that are fragile and can easily be broken by another female passerby. Her emotional needs are simply better served by one faithful and dedicated lover than by many who come and go. Therefore, it is very alien to her way of thinking to see anything appealing in raw and indiscriminate sex. It is much more in her interest to glorify and romanticize the sexual act. She has sensitized herself more thoroughly to a stimulus called "love," than to a mere sexual cue. "Love" simply has vastly more power.

Sex, to a girl, may become a very valid currency. It can be traded for affection. It is like buying insurance for one's sexual identity: one pays a premium reluctantly, hoping it will pay off generously in emotional dividends. A girl firms up her sexual role by securing and holding a man's love. Her ego demands that she establish herself firmly in a loving relationship. Just as a boy may test his capacity by the notches on his bedpost, a girl tests her capacity by how deeply she can fall in love, or, more importantly, how deeply she can make her partner fall in love with her.

Talking love and trading sex therefore mean different things to males and females in our world. On one side, love talk is the price to pay to score a sexual victory. On the other side, it is a price to extract for emotional affiliation.

Perhaps the preceding chapter was a little harsh on boys, characterizing them as selfish, self-seeking, presumptuous, greedy, and unfeeling. Now it's the ladies' turn to hear what they do sexually to internalize a feminine role. There is a price to be paid when sex is seen as a bartering device that is used by the girl for her own emotional ends.

A girl learns early that sex is an exploitative, manipulative, competitive tool—she could have no better controlling device at her command. Whereas he needs to prove himself openly, she need only sit back and pull the strings:

> "I teased him all through the social studies period. I crossed my legs and his ears went pink. I let my tongue run over my lips and his eyes got this drugged look. I pretended to be hot and started unbuttoning the top of my blouse— he actually started to tremble, the poor, silly guy."

Many girls think nothing of using sex for emotional blackmail by saying: "All right . . . if you tell me you love me"; ". . . if you stay with me"; ". . . if you promise not to leave me." Intercourse, when happening this way, may have tremendous psychological dividends: a genuine assurance of being loved and needed, or the knowledge of having taken a risk at being rejected and having won, or the feelings of having used one's sexual powers to one's advantage. Girls, too, keep a constant watch on their self-esteem, and making it sexually can prove all kinds of things!

Most girls know all too well the double standard of our culture which permits a boy to lay as many girls as he pleases and still claim a virgin for his bride. It gets a girl into a double bind: she feels offended if he makes a pass at her, and hurt if he does not. If he can't be tempted by her female charm, she feels unlovable; and if he is, she feels herself to be a sexual commodity. It is therefore very much to her advantage to let him struggle with a double-edged temptation—his need to have sex, and his fear of losing control to her by yielding to her demands for love. A success in love is a very personal victory.

However, it takes some willingness to learn conniving. A girl can learn that there is virtue in limited giving, that there are rewards for being tricky, that subtle and preventive tactics can go a long way in keeping a boy in high suspense without letting him score. A girl, before she is married, is always aware of a dual purpose in her relationships with a boy: she has to keep his desire at peak and his actual accomplishments low. She has to permit enough petting to sustain and to hold his interest. At the same time she has to keep her body needs under control in order to have a tight grip on her currency. She may tempt him mercilessly, with no intention of letting him win. And why should she? She weakens her currency if she does—there's inflation in the sexual market as well. He may or may not know that her need for dates is a lever in his behalf. She is aware at all times that she is responsible for being both tempting and forbidding. She knows she can force him into emotional concessions against his will.

This trading off of sexual favors may lead to learning which may be hurtful to a later marriage relationship. It could logically be said that the more successful a girl is in avoiding intercourse before marriage, the less prepared she may be for genuine abandon in the sexual bed. She has trained herself for many years to hold off physically while charging up emotionally, just as he has trained himself for a long time that it is to his advantage to feel a certain detachment when engaging in sex.

What we have, then, is a situation in which both sexes are "boxed in" by their respective sexual roles. Each role is somewhat of a distortion and a caricature. Sexual roles serve needs, but they do make for built-in constraints. A male will be careful to abstain from expressing his gentler emotions; there's too much at stake for him if he does. He loses his right to be in control, to be in command. Boys can easily come to feel that the price is far too high; they may choose to starve themselves emotionally rather than risk their manhood by showing that they care. Emotional involvements are simply not in their interests, they restrict their movements and thereby weaken their ego. Many myths, ancient and current, pick this up. Some people in Mexico believe to this day that even animals will feel contempt for a man in love and will despise him for his weakness. A deer, for example, will gleefully sidestep a snare set by a man in love, snorting disdainfully, "Pooh-pooh" while doing so.

Many males, therefore, in order to avoid feeling threatened, will make love as quickly and uninvolvedly as possible. But time and patience and tenderness are just what a woman needs if she is to feel that their sexual union is satisfying on the emotional level. So quickness and roughness make intercourse less successful, and this in turn aggravates a man's fear that he is not very good. The man, having had fleeting, hurried relations, leaves the woman just when she wants to be given more attention, making her frustrated and furious, for which she blames him, for which he feels more inadequate, which makes him more anxious about the relationship, more hurried the next time, and so on. And a woman, not understanding why a man would recoil from too heavy emotional demands, will say the wrong things: "Stay with me." "Don't leave me!" "Don't you love me anymore?" He, having been taught all his life to be on guard about things emotional and about things feminine, can hardly be expected to relax under such psychological siege. His need is to protect his inner world from emotional invasion, the very thing she is out to get.

So it's a hurtful tug-of-war: it may be just as difficult for a man to expose himself through words of love as it is for a woman to strip to nakedness before a man without reluctance and fear and shame. Words of tenderness come easier to most women than to men; freedom of body and action seems simpler to men. Both call for an abandoning of facades and fronts, however, and both leave one vulnerable and at the mercy of the partner.

8

THE TWO-FACED COIN

Mixed Sexual Emotions

When two people are under the spell of romantic love, the whole world will be seen through rose-colored glasses. Each considers the other to possess more than mortal perfection. Each is convinced that their union is going to be one life-long stretch of never-ending bliss. There is so much newness and wonder and magic in the relationship that everything one partner does is cherished by the other. Lovers are truly "bewitched" human beings; they are deeply convinced that their love for each other is of such nature that other feelings—emotions of hate and destruction—could never possibly arise.

However, no sexual involvement is a simple and clear-cut relationship. For one, emotions connected with falling in love are of very great intensity, and for that reason alone may be difficult to sustain. Our emotional machinery is not designed for an unlimited capacity for ecstasy. People very much in love can irritate each other beyond belief. Clothes are left on the bathroom floor, appointments and promises are forgotten, hair curlers and face cream or an unshaven beard can set the lovers' teeth on edge. Or suddenly, "out of nowhere," there appears a third party in the picture, and jealousy strikes hard at the core of one's self. Feelings of love and affection can turn into wishes to hurt and be hurt.

Love can bring pain. And sex can mean cruelty. When we look at sex, it is striking to see how much of it has very hurtful elements. Our language reflects how we frequently think about sex—how much of our feelings express anger and cruelty and hurtfulness. A pregnant girl has been "knocked up." A car engine or a business deal has been "screwed up." We talk of "sex and violence" in movies as if these two were naturally the same. These words and expressions would not be used if the sexual act were always thought of as something beautiful and gentle. The choice of words shows that often we feel anything *but* kind and loving when we speak of "making love."

The causes for hostility in sex are explained by psychologists in different ways. Some see it as an "inborn" tendency, as a manifestation of remnant feelings from ancient times when caveman had to be on guard even in his most unguarded moments. During copulation, prehistoric man was defenseless for a while and therefore more vulnerable to attack.

In order to keep the adrenaline in his bloodstream at a high enough level for him to be able to react quickly to outside provocation and threat, caveman had to maintain feelings of aggression and rage during intercourse. His survival depended on it. Interlocked and mixed feelings of love, tenderness, and caring on one hand, and rage, hatred, and aggression on the other are therefore seen as our evolutionary heritage from a distant past.

Freud, who was concerned with explaining the psychological defense mechanisms of our self, developed a different theory. He attributed much of the aggression we see in sex to the manifestation of "penis envy" and "castration anxiety"—terms we have briefly introduced before. Freud speculated that when a little boy discovers that he possesses a sexual organ which is missing in a girl, he concludes that she has "lost" her penis or that it was cut off as punishment. The boy will naturally develop a fear that the same thing will somehow happen to him if he doesn't look out for himself. Parents may exaggerate this fear by threatening to cut off the boy's penis, perhaps in a joking manner, perhaps as a threat when they discover him masturbating.

Little girls, according to Freud, may actually be very jealous of the boy's equipment and may really wish to cut it off. A previous chapter has mentioned that many men carry through life a hidden fear that girls are "out to get them." A male may actually come to think of the vagina as a snapping, biting, scissoring thing that may hurt his penis. Fantasies of the "vagina with teeth" are reported by psychotherapists in several countries.

More recent psychological writers have cast doubt on the belief that these fears hold true in all countries and among all people, and questioned whether they are even relevant in the lives of most normal people. But it is impossible to deny that in some extreme cases men may have very strong anxieties about castration, and women strong penis envy. Whether the need to hurt or be hurt is based on early childhood anxiety and sexual envy or not, it is a fact that many men experience rage as a result of being "weakened" by a woman through intercourse. Similarly, many women experience a deep unconscious hatred against men which makes it difficult for them to submit to sex unless it is in a form that will severely and cruelly hurt the male.

Still other psychologists think that there are meaningful but "incidental" reasons why hurting is attached to intercourse. A male, for example, may have a persistent, though often unconscious, anger toward his mother. This feeling can spread to women in general, and specifically toward his sexual partner. Hence, one way of expressing anger toward mother is to hurt the sexual partner. On the other extreme, a man may be so attached to his mother in a mixed-up sexual way that he cannot have intercourse with a woman he respects because she reminds him of his mother. Others who have associated anger and hate with sex cannot have intercourse with a woman they deeply love because they cannot bear inflicting "pain" on their beloved. A girl may unconsciously wish to hurt her partner for favors reluctantly given. And a male, of course, can hurt a female by getting her pregnant if she is not his wife, or when she is but does not want a pregnancy. Some girls may even refuse to use contraceptives out of a hidden wish to hurt.

> "I knew I took a chance, but I could not bring myself to go to the drugstore. . . . I made my boyfriend seduce me. I seduced him into seducing me. When I found out I was pregnant, I blamed him."

To have a baby "by accident" is a way to hurt rather permanently. This is suggested by the expression "to trap a man." A trapped animal is a hurt animal. It can be a source of severe humiliation for a boy to have the whole community know that he is the one responsible for a pregnancy.

More modern theories lean toward the belief that sadism
—the wish to hurt sexually—involves a strong craving for
mastery. A sadistic partner enjoys a helpless, suffering mate
who can be used sexually in any hurtful way. Much of
deviant sexuality contains elements of hurting. Sexual assault, rape, mutilation, pedophilia, incest—all have ingredients of aggression. There are some men who claim they can
achieve their maximum gratification only by severely
wounding or even killing women. Murder, for example,
sometimes involves carving up a woman's body in a specifically sexual way. Even setting fires can be a sadistic way of
finding sexual release: for some people, there is something
frightfully powerful and sexually arousing in a raging fire
out of control.

Many perfectly average men and women, too, enjoy intercourse more when it contains strong elements of pain.
Biting or scratching the partner, or liking to have it done,
is part of the sexual repertoire of many couples who are by
no means abnormal. Quite hard and painful biting may be
a way of "playful teasing." This may partly be a matter of
the sheer physical sensations involved; it is possible to
heighten and intensify arousal by pressure or pain or even
constriction and bondage. But it also seems to involve the
wish to hurt and be hurt. Taken to extremes, the desire to
hurt in a savage way or be hurt by cruelty can rightfully be
called a perversion. A sadistic man may beat his partner with
a whip or chain or cut her with a knife before intercourse;
a woman who "enjoys" being mutilated in this way is said
to have a masochistic need. Of course, women may also be
sadistic, and men may have masochistic tendencies.

On a more hidden emotional level, sadistic needs can
take on very subtle shades. A man who is afraid of losing

out in the competition with a woman, who wants to be "on top" and to dominate and control, and who is very angry with women for being as powerful as they are, may have strong reasons for wanting to be hurtful in intercourse. Many psychologists believe that men frequently associate the penis with a knife or gun in their thinking, at least unconsciously. There is some evidence which suggests strongly that many men think of their sexual organ in this manner—as a weapon that has the power to explode and hurt or to rip and cut or in some other way inflict injury and pain. They may have fantasies of intercourse where the sexual act becomes a sort of attack on a woman. Sometimes this wish finds symbolic expression. Some gun clubs have rest rooms lettered "Pistols" and "Holsters"—this may be a covert and "cute" way of expressing hostility in sex.

There are many women who think of intercourse as primarily a painful, ripping, damaging experience, often as a result of having been warned by their mothers. Or they may be afraid of all the hurtful *consequences* that men may do to them in connection with intercourse—for example, of becoming pregnant, of being raped, of being treated harshly and roughly, of being "loved and left." When women are afraid of the whole sexual process, it is usually hard to tell how much of their fear is fear of failure, how much is fear of being punished for something wicked, and how much is fear of being hurt by the sexual act itself. And when a male will use his penis in such a way as to suggest physical harm, and will have sex in anger and in a rough and hurtful manner, it is easy for a female to feel that she is being raped against her will. Similarly, a girl who is always looking at boys as competitors, always trying to get the best of them and to be "on top" in other areas of life, may find it very difficult to relax and stop competing and lie still in the sexual relationship. She, too, may have strong reasons to want to hurt her lover with sex.

She may, for example, want to lead him into sexual misconduct and than stand aloof and laugh. It is very gratifying for some girls—even girls who do not enjoy intercourse at all—to have boys make passes at them.

> "I used sex as a bait. . . . I never promised him outright, but I let him think I was considering it at least. He kept bugging me, and I enjoyed pretending that I was greatly confused and tempted."

Often, such a girl successful in provoking a boy to have intercourse with her will then act very righteous afterward and will blame the boy—by the way she acts, or by what she says to him or others—for all that has happened. Many a girl who enjoys tempting a boy mercilessly will after a while pull her robes of virtue around her, stand tall, and accuse *him* of having wicked intentions. The foregoing routine is sometimes described as "leading the boy on and then cutting him off." Freudian thinking would hold that such expression has at least an undertone of castration. If a girl tries to arouse a boy without intending to go through with the sexual act, it is a subtle form of hurtful, sadistic behavior, although we tend to think that there is nothing wrong with it.

Masochism, the wish to be hurt sexually, seems the reverse of what we said before of the motivational forces behind human behavior. In general, human beings seem compelled to seek pleasure and to avoid pain. A masochistic individual prefers things the other way around—he seeks out pain and avoids pleasure.

An individual who likes to be hurt sexually often harbors

deep hidden feelings of inferiority and powerlessness. In addition, it seems that in a masochistic personality there are deep feelings of hate and resentment against the sexual partner. Such hate is hard to admit openly, however, for it places the self in a vulnerable position. Not very many people can live with a sexual involvement that has hate as its main element.

The self, therefore, in order to survive emotionally, invents a reason. Masochism can be seen as a somewhat bizarre means of getting rid of a conflict that is threatening to the self. By submitting to someone big and strong and powerful who has all control, the self is released from having to face up to its true feelings. By surrendering as a "slave" to a "master," it obtains a form of "suffering protection." Masochistic people will often greatly pride themselves on "loving" the partner despite cruel and continuous torment over a very long period of time. It is not always "selfish" sex that pays the biggest emotional dividends.

Of such complexity are our emotions that it is often hard to tell apart just how much hurting we sometimes want to do and how deeply we want to be hurt. Let's take jealousy, for example, as an expression of sadomasochistic feelings—an *emotional mixture* of wanting to hurt and be hurt. There are forces deep within us—powerful hidden furies and fears—that make us behave in sadomasochistic ways when jealousy takes hold of us.

> "I knew it the minute he showed up with his brand-new Honda that I had lost Brenda to him. Even though not a word was said by either one of us, I knew it in my guts by the way she looked at him, all flushed and lovely . . . and by the way she suddenly looked at me, as if she wished me

on the moon. I felt like slashing his tires . . . in fact, I
fantasized for a long time about how I would loosen a bolt
so he would get killed in an accident."

Jealousy is a reaction to a blow to one's sexual prestige.
It can be seen as a blow to one's mastery in the sexual arena.
A jealous person has suffered a psychological loss. A nox-
ious stimulus has come into conflict with the vulnerable self,
and a reaction must take place because the psychic balance
is upset. If one's body gets sick, a number of complicated
processes begin to speed up to do away with the "intruder"
and to restore the body to health. If a virus, for example,
is contracted by the body, reproduction of white blood cells
is increased to combat the infection. Blood temperature is
raised. Liquid intake becomes more urgent. Appetite falls
off. Fatigue sets in. All this takes place on an automatic level
—a number of intricate defense mechanisms are rallied to
combat the "villain" that is a threat to one's health.

A similar reaction seems to take place in a "jealousy
attack." An intruder has appeared on the scene, challenging
the self. We all like to think of ourselves as persons with
virtues and assets greater than what any rival could possibly
have to offer to our love. Even though a relationship may
not even have been greatly valued until it was lost, jealousy
strikes hard when someone else invades our sexual terrain.
The self has no choice but to react to provocation. It seems
reasonable to assume that the ego will react to frustration
in proportion to its magnitude—a strong reaction to strong
provocation, and a mild reaction to a mild threat. The violence with which human beings react in jealousy would
seem to suggest that much is at stake here indeed.

In the light of the previous chapters, this should not be

too hard to understand. One's love is a very precious commodity; there is a wealth of invested emotions. Jealous lovers tend to act as if they had a license for emotional hoarding. They are the stingiest people, they are not about to share their "commodity" even one tiny bit, for sharing would diminish their precious possession.

We have a tongue-in-cheek saying that in love, as in war, the end justifies the means. It is important to keep the rival away at any cost, by force or by cunning or deceit. It is almost as if by attacking the rival, the self is prevented from attacking itself: "If I can hurt my rival fast and good, I am not as likely to feel the bitter pain of rejection." A thwarted self is an emotional fury on the warpath. It has to destroy or face being destroyed emotionally. Driven by a tormenting image of affections "wasted" on somebody else, the ego is out to kill! No means is too contemptuous to force the rival out into the cold and to lure the straying lover back into one's possession. When jealous people speak of love, they mean getting it, not giving it.

Yet, for all its violence and fierceness, jealousy has also strong elements of masochism—willing submission to suffering for the sake of one's love. For how can we explain that those love relationships which hurt the most, which bring the most anguish and tears and loneliness and disappointments and frustrations—anything but happiness—are the ones we cling to the hardest? A love that comes easy is not nearly as tempting as one that has poisonous thorns. Why do we struggle and strive and connive for "advantages" that should really make us blush, if only we could get hold of our senses? Why do we remain attached to "loves" that may be very hurtful to our self? Seldom are we willing to replace a lost love with someone else when wounds are raw and smarting, even though doing so would certainly bring us relief. In principle, the anguish of jealousy is not all that different from the "pleasures" of masochistic feelings.

So we have looked at love in yet another way: as a strange and mixed-up emotion which can—at the same time!—feel like the sweetest thing in the world, and the bitterest.

9

KIDS IN CRADLES

Products of Hidden Needs

Intercourse makes babies! Sex can lead to parenthood. And much like a mousetrap, a prison, and a coffin, parenthood is easier to get into than out of. It is impossible to send babies back from where they came. Therefore, a central message of this chapter will be that a baby should be a baby and not an emotional accident.

When lovers become parents, either intentionally or against their will, they usually expect that a baby will bring them nothing but sheer joy. Folklore has it that "sex, marriage, and children" is the package that guarantees a well-rounded, satisfying life. In the social learning that takes place, we absorb the image of the family as the "happy unit," the nucleus of stability, the one place of safety for a person's emotional anchorage in an ever-changing world. On Thanksgiving, at Christmas time, on Mother's Day, we pay homage to our belief that there are built-in rewards for parenthood.

Note these statements against the above frame of reference:

> "I was scared silly all through my pregnancy. I did not know what to expect, and I'm a coward when it comes to pain. Besides, I felt rotten. . . . I was throwing up, and aching, and weepy, and just plain *miserable.* The only thing that kept me going was the thought that once I held my baby in my arms, I would be miraculously rewarded for all that misery. And then I held Tommy, and I felt *nothing.* I looked at my baby and saw how red and ugly and wrinkled he was, and I felt betrayed and double-crossed. I thought: Big deal!"

> "I *know* that I don't want any children at all. I love life too much to let myself be cheated out of twenty or so years by diapers, dishes, PTAs, and soap operas. I want to travel, I want to *live* my life. I have talent, I am intelligent, I want to *make* something of myself. Children would be a disaster. . . . I would be a disaster as a mother."

> "I always wanted to be an artist. I was living with paints and brushes by the time I was four. My parents went through considerable sacrifice to send me to college so I could be an art major. I had so many dreams. When I met Sue in my junior year, I thought I had found the girl who could share my dreams with me. She seemed to understand; she was artistic, too. We wanted only one child . . . maybe two. Now we have five. I still paint. Fences and gutters."

This is a new tune in contemporary America. Often it is perceived as a discord, as springing from the minds of somewhat twisted personalities. However, it is a tune that strikes a raw nerve in many a young parent today. Several years ago, Ellen Peck wrote *The Baby Trap,* a book that became a hot best seller overnight. It must have had a strong message with which frustrated parents could identify.

This chapter will look briefly at our assumptions about parenthood and sex. Then it will highlight the psychological pressures that work in favor of having babies or against having any. Finally, it will conclude with some thoughts as to what would happen if we were to shift emotional gears and redirect our values and beliefs regarding parenthood in the opposite direction.

"Population explosion" has become a household term that evokes a mental picture of "standing room only." Even first-graders in our schools are already aware of the fear which many people have that we will "breed ourselves right out of existence." Statistics and charts tell us how rapidly we multiply. The media tell us we are depleting our natural resources. The energy crisis is already here. It seems as if the threat of overpopulation has always been around.

However, we have not always felt this way.

It is a striking phenomenon of very recent times that we seem willing to block and prevent potential life, or even— as happens in abortion—terminate life once it has started. Fertility today has taken on offensive connotations in many people's thinking. Yet relics from prehistoric times emphasize the tremendous importance of fertility. Indeed, in many instances, religion was synonymous with fertility, and the gods who had control over giving or denying new life were the ones most worshiped and most feared. Many primitive people believed the moon to be the father of all children, and great reverence was paid to women for their role in bearing the offspring of a tribe. Some people speculate that a total reversal of social power took place when it was finally discovered that a man could beget very many children in a very short span of time, while a woman could bear only one each year. At that time, women lost their supreme status: men became the lords and masters, and women were designated to a secondary place.

Our own Judeo-Christian tradition stresses heavily the virtues of parenthood. The first couple in the Garden of Eden received the order from the Creator: "Be fruitful, and multiply, and replenish the earth" (Gen. 1: 28). Abraham was promised that his offspring would be "as the stars of the heaven, and as the sand which is upon the seashore" (Gen. 22:17). Biblical writings saw barrenness as a terrible calamity. Conception was often portrayed as happening under miraculous circumstances, against incredible odds and cunning conspiracies of fate.

Emotionally, we still tend to think along these lines, even though fertility in our times is no longer seen as a very desirable thing. We firmly believe, for example, that parenthood will magically transform very ordinary men and women to act in certain unselfish ways, in spite of overwhelming evidence to the contrary. We believe that having children brings vastly more joy than not having any. We assert that those who cannot have children—or worse, do not choose to have any—are unfulfilled, unhappy, have warped character traits, are selfish, neurotic, and queer. We go farther than that and believe that an *only* child inherits the "curse" that is on his parents, so that he in turn will develop in selfish and spoiled and other undesirable ways. Until very recently, wanting one child was almost as unheard of as wanting none.

We unthinkingly believe that children, by their mere presence, will deepen and enrich a sexual relationship. Cou-

ples who are sterile will often turn to adoption or artificial
insemination in the belief that their sexual union is incomplete—that children are necessary to a happy married life.
Marital strife is often blamed on the lack of children. Men
feel threatened by infertility, thinking it reflects on their
virility. Now as in the past, men have proudly taken credit
for having a large family and especially many boys, but often
refused to share the blame for a childless union. Women,
too, may feel miraculously elevated by motherhood, since
babies are "living proof" that men found them desirable. If
pregnancy does not result, heartache can be profound.

> "Bill and I tried for a baby for years. I held my breath
> each time my period was late, hoping and praying that this
> time it would work. Bill was beginning to blame me, saying
> he had read somewhere that tenseness could prevent a preg-
> nancy. I was tense, all right. . . . I cried my eyes out when
> I was alone."

There are many motivational forces working on our
psyche that may push us to wish for a child.

Becoming a parent may be a tremendous step for an
insecure person to establish an identity of his own. By caring
for a baby, dependency needs are met, and by identifying
with the baby, one cares for oneself. Suddenly an insignifi-
cant woman has a *role* with built-in stability—especially a
woman who does not have ready access to education, satisfying employment, or other gratifying roles. Having power
and control over another human being—even if only a very
tiny one—can be vastly gratifying for some women, even
more so if they perceive the baby to be a weapon of covert
control over the father as well.

Other dependent young wives may see a baby as cementing their marriage into greater strength. They hope for deeper companionship with their mates, the child's needs being their common ground of interest. With a baby in the house, the wife hopes her husband will become more loving, more concerned, more mature, less prone to "straying from the hearth."

There is also the romantic aspect of having a baby born of a union of love—the wonder and awe that comes with this creation. A baby is said to increase in weight six billion times from the moment of conception to the time it is born. There can be a profound feeling of pride and accomplishment in having had part in such a miracle. For many women it is the only worthwhile contribution to mankind they perceive as ever having made. It is a very personal and intimate thing; and self-worth, especially in a sexual way, is firmly tied to giving life to another human being.

Then there are the changing physical features of pregnancy which give many women a truly euphoric sensation. It is easy to get "high" on a pregnancy. The fuller breasts, the roundness of hips and abdomen, the gentle kicking and moving of the growing fetus, can give a very lovely feeling of motherhood. Men too are subject to the emotional "spell" of pregnancy. Some men "participate" in a pregnancy to the extent that they too experience the by-products of carrying a baby: morning sickness, craving for the proverbial pickle, even imaginary labor pains which are perceived as real and very painful. Pregnancy always affects a sexual relationship—sometimes in rather unexpected ways.

There are other, more hidden, motivational forces that may steer a couple toward a pregnancy. There might be a need to compete with same-sex parents, or to spite parents, or to force a reluctant lover into marriage, or to hurt a sex partner, or literally to "inject" a shaky sexual relationship with "new life."

In Freudian thinking, a pregnancy seems desirable because a girl wants a baby as a penis substitute, or because she wants to go through childbearing as "atonement" for having sinned sexually, or because a masochistic need is satisfied by a lifelong state of slavery and suffering for one's child. The myth of the selfless, suffering, sacrificing mother finds many versions in literature and art.

When we come to the *negative* aspects of parenthood, we are far more reluctant to express our real and genuine feelings. Parents do not as a rule admit with emotional ease they are sorry they created a new human life. It is customary to pretend great happiness and satisfaction for having made a baby, despite the fact that the costs and burdens of parenthood can be staggering, emotionally and otherwise.

Typically, a first baby is a most severe shock to a sexual relationship—all the more severe because it is so little expected. A pregnancy causes drastic weight and figure changes in the woman, changes that many men perceive as very repulsive. Varicose veins, nausea and vomiting at the most unlikely times and inappropriate places, mood swings, loss of sexual interest, the sudden appearance of unexpected and less than pleasant character traits—all this can be bitter wear and tear on a sexual relationship accustomed to serenity and beauty. In our youth-and-beauty-conscious world, women often suffer from periods of severe depression during pregnancy as they begin to take on the characteristics of an older woman: loss of girlish figure, sluggishness of movement, shortness of breath, swollen feet, brittle and glossless hair. Folk wisdom claims that "every baby costs a tooth." Many a woman feels the baby inside her to be an actual parasite—living off the mother's body and sapping her strength and beauty.

Fear of childbirth itself terrorizes many women. Delivery is often seen as a journey through the Valley of Death, from which there is no reprieve and no return. A woman may turn against her partner, blaming him for the pregnancy. A man may feel responsible for the pain he has "inflicted" upon his partner, and will feel helpless and angry for not being able to share in the process of birth. A man, too, may be terror-stricken, and may want to "undo" what he has done.

An insecure husband may react to his wife's pregnancy with jealousy and misgivings, fearing that the child will take his place in *his* woman's affection. His need to be mothered may be so strong that he resents the child even after it is born, although usually he will repress such feelings and feel very guilty about having them.

When the baby arrives, the full impact of the little tyrant is felt by the consternated couple. No past learning has prepared them for what is now to come. Young parents, accustomed to being absorbed in each other and the aesthetic experience of their love, suddenly find themselves confronted with mess, noise, confusion, an upset daily routine, diapers, howling screams in the middle of the night, and hourly emergencies that fray each other's nerves. There is probably no parent alive who has not at one time or another resented this massive intrusion into his formerly so peaceful life. Yet hostility is rarely openly expressed, and mixed feelings about being a parent only in carefully veiled terms.

Feelings of resentment and jealousy run deep, however. There is fear that the honeymoon has come to a permanent

and grinding halt. Children cut down on many activities.
Vacations have to be postponed or canceled altogether.
Parties have to be bypassed. Friends who are single and
"free" begin to stay away. Even at home, sexual pleasure
seems constantly interrupted by the little intruder. Hus-
bands complain bitterly that their wives are too tired for sex
before falling asleep, yet jump out of bed—fully awake!—
at the slightest stirring or whimper from the crib. What was
expected to be a joy from heaven begins to look conspicu-
ously like a trap, and the smaller and more numerous the
children, the more secure and permanent a trap it seems to
be.

The bulk of a couple's married life is spent living with
their children. Most couples "welcome" their first baby in
less than two years' time after the wedding bells have rung.
For the mother, especially, there follows right on the heels
of romance and honeymoon a decade or so of acute and
monotonous confinement. Her interests become so focused
on the children that often no real communication with her
husband can take place. And what makes this matter worse
is that our culture gives a woman no legitimate means of
voicing this resentment. She is not permitted to say she hates
her prison. She cannot say she is raving mad at her little
tormentors who break her new dishes and throw up all over
the carpets and flush her slippers down the toilet. She is
expected to "enjoy the children while they are still young"
and is labeled a monster—and will perceive herself as such
—if she doesn't. Women must learn to adjust to this state
of restriction or suffer bitter social ostracism. There is much
merit in some women's assertion that a quarter century
of their lives tied to children, diapers, the house, school
lunches, PTAs, car pools, and soap operas, and the resulting

frustration, boredom, and loss of self-esteem, are too high a price to pay for motherhood.

Men, too, may find children a bitter stress on their emotional resources. Before babies arrived on the scene, virility and manhood meant adequacy in the sexual bed—an activity that could be described as fun. Now being a "real man" means being an adequate provider. Children are a very costly acquisition. A sizable "down payment" at delivery, periodic "installments" over some twenty-five years covering doctor and dentist bills, food, entertainment, bikes, summer camps, clothes and shoes, will drain and deplete a father's pocketbook and restrict his freedom severely. There is also the indirect loss of income because the mother cannot work. Children are a hindrance to one's quest for success—they take away money, time, and emotional strength that could be devoted to "greater" things. For many men, it's either success or children: and often their male ego is firmly tied to success.

Nevertheless, childlessness—as a choice—is often ruled out. If couples wish they were childless, such wishes are usually repressed into the unconscious, especially if children are already born. Many parents equate such wishes with death wishes and find it too frightening and painful to see themselves in that light. Sometimes they project their wishes onto the couples who openly don't wish or plan for children, accusing *them* of being selfish and abnormal and less than adequate sexually.

Most men and women don't feel a clear pull in either direction, but wish for—and fear—both sides of both worlds. Some women feel a strong rejection of the feminine role that is built into motherhood. At the same time, they feel an equally strong need to be found attractive and lovable and worthy of a man's sexual attraction. Many see their children as valuable permanent links of affection to the man they love. But they also know that children mean a chaotic house and a loss of that special feeling of intimacy that came with first sex. Children may be secretly seen as nuisance to be avoided, yet pressure in our culture is such that it is hard to resist such typical remarks: "When *are* you going to have children?" "Don't you *like* children?" "Won't you be *lonely* when you get older?" "*Everyone* wants children." In order not to be labeled immature, selfish, unnatural, and sick emotionally, couples find it easier to say apologetically: "We don't want one *just yet.*" If they are more courageous, they might add timidly: "We aren't absolutely *sure* we want them ever." Few will say simply: "We want no children" and let it go at that.

Yet from the point of view of emotional health and sexual satisfaction, many arguments could be made in favor of deciding against—or at least postponing—the arrival of a child. For the first time in human history, contraceptives have made it possible to enjoy sex without having to fear a pregnancy. This is such a new thought in our world that we have not yet adjusted our value systems to this important scientific advancement. It is almost as if we are wearing clothes no longer suited to a certain climate.

Here are some of the ideas that have sprung up in the realm of "birth control":

What would happen, for example, if children were brought up in such a way that they would not *expect* to become parents? Childless couples would then be the "normal" ones and those who wanted children would be "disturbed." Career-oriented women would take their rightful place in line with the most successful men. Professional and artistic pursuits would be increased. Women would feel young much longer, since they would not have to equate age with menopause. It is conceivable that marriage as we know it today would disappear, since marriage is primarily an institution to safeguard the rearing of the young. Instead, friendships would be formed that would place emphasis on emotional compatibility and sexual fit.

These changes, and many others, are not as strange as they may seem. They may even become necessary as we adjust to the changes that the contraceptive revolution is bound to bring. Just as parents can be taught that it is natural to want and to have children, they can be taught to see that there are many disadvantages to parenthood. Some of these changes in value orientation are already taking place. Especially in college populations, there often is a great reluctance to enter a marriage contract, even though deep and genuine love binds the partners to each other. Many young men and women now choose a life-style more to their liking and closer to their emotional well-being, and feel comfortable in roles other than parenthood. Many decide on a trial marriage whereby sex is openly permitted and practiced, but having babies is strongly tabooed. The feared threat of becoming an "old maid" seems to have totally disappeared: an unmarried woman now sees herself as a vivacious, zestful "swinging chick."

If choice is ours at all, this is an area where clear, rational, unemotional choice is needed. A baby is all too easy to come by. Parenthood can be accomplished in a matter of minutes, but once accomplished, it is there to stay for a very long time

—a lifetime, in some cases. A choice for or against parent-hood is a tremendously important decision, and one that should not be left to emotions or whims or the glitter of a star-studded night.

10

WARFARE ON BED AND BOARD

Women's Liberation

In the past it was customary for a girl to be "given" into marriage by her father or an older brother—handed over from one male into the care of the next. She would not walk down the aisle to take the man of her choice, strong and self-confident, all by herself. The wedding ceremony made her "his better half"; with the exchange of rings, she became "Mrs. William D." or "Mrs. Robert R." Physically and symbolically, she renounced any claim to an identity of her own and surrendered to her husband's "superiority."

Once she was married, her life-span was defined by three boundaries: *"Kinder, Küche, und Kirche"*—children, kitchen, and the church. A "good" wife and mother was proud to be humble. She would try hard to be helpless and sweet, expecting the strong male to solve her dilemmas for her, avoiding images that she thought to be unfeminine, such as striving for power, or having a will and an opinion of her

own, or asserting her own intelligence and strength of conviction. She would adapt to his life-style; never would he
adapt to hers. Once a girl was married, she was assured—
or so the myth of marital happiness goes—that she would
know no greater worry than the wax shine on her kitchen
floor.

Is this really the woman of the past? In a way one could
say that she is, although the stereotype is still very much
with us today. For it is just a few years ago that there arrived
—by the busloads—a large number of furious women on
the steps of Atlantic City's Convention Hall. Outside on the
sidewalks, with television cameras focused on their flaming,
angry faces, these women made it very clear that they had
come to announce their break with tradition. They threw
their bras, false eyelashes, issues of *True Romance, Playboy*
magazines, and steno pads into a "Freedom Trash Can" and
set it all on fire, making known to the world their outrage
at being treated as "chattel"—as mindless property of men.
No longer, they protested, would they tolerate the "degrading, boob-girlie symbolism" which was perpetuated in the
crowning of a beauty queen—Miss America of 1968.

Today's young people cannot afford to grow up and step
into sexual adulthood without taking a hard, questioning
look at this new wave of articulate women who protest
against their image as a sexual object for the sole pleasure
of the male. These women insist upon their intelligence and
talent and dignity as *human beings* and demand to be treated
as man's equal and not as his ignorant "possession" over
which he has power and control.

Women's Lib has caused much controversy in America.
It is a new and inflammatory movement and by no means
always popular with the average American woman—much

less the American male. It represents, nevertheless, a most significant development. Its spokesmen are women who, many people feel, tend to overstate their cause in order to get the attention of the world and make known to everyone the nature of their grievances.

The issues being raised, however, do not pertain to women's liberation alone. They should be seen as having merit to *human* liberation. For the division of sexual roles —with the man strictly playing the strong, aggressive, hard-headed, unemotional partner, and the woman adhering to the role of a helpless, submissive, easily swayed, soft-hearted, playful child—has taken its toll in human misery very much on both sides of the fence. It is an unnatural division in many ways in that it forces upon individuals certain patterns of behavior and thinking very harmful to a genuine and loving relationship. It comes with a price tag that many couples no longer care to pay.

Here are some of the issues raised by Women's Lib:

Even the best form of marriage, they say, is just as good as slavery. A marriage contract forces women into lifelong servitude to their families—no labor could be had more cheaply in America. For sooner or later every woman realizes this: no matter how good her marriage might be, it is a common form of "making a living," and often a very miserly living at that. A woman is dependent for food and shelter on her husband, for which he fully expects to be paid in the sexual bed.

"Tom would get up from the supper table and say with a yawn: 'All right, dearie, let's have a roll in the hay.' In the morning he would reach for me, groaning: 'Another one of those days—let's get our batteries charged up before we

tackle it.' In between, he would say: 'Let's hurry up and do
some balling—I promised the boys I'd go fishing with
them.' I was nothing to him but a body he could use whenever he felt the need.''

The women's liberation movement claims that many hus-
bands have learned to see their wives as nothing but vessels
for the male seed, that rape—intercourse against one's
wishes—is committed more often inside marriage than outside its boundaries, and that even prostitution is in principle
preferable to the state of being married, since at least it gives
a woman an *option* to choose or refuse a partner's sexual
demands. In marriage, they assert, a woman is expected
night after night to minister to a man's sexual demands—
often against her will, without remuneration or considera-
tion for her feelings or concern for her body and soul.

"I feel most comfortable sleeping on my stomach, with
my arms around the pillow. If Jack wanted sex at night, he
would place his hot hand between my shoulderblades. It
never occurred to him to let me know in any other way. I
came to dislike that hand on my back so much I turned to
ice the moment I felt it on my skin. It was such a little thing,
but it killed my love for him. I could never bring myself to
tell him that. Sometimes I think that our marriage would
have survived with the tiniest bit of imagination on his
part.''

There are other indignities to marriage, aside from being
forced to give sex as a matter of duty and on instant command. For example, motherhood is commonly thought of as
the supreme career for any woman—but only *married* motherhood. Motherhood per se is not supreme by any means,
as any unwed girl discovers all too soon. If motherhood

were sacred in and of itself, a girl should not have to suffer society's rejection if she is not married while having a child. One of the strongest goals of Women's Lib is that every woman be given control over her own body: to have a baby if and when she wants a child, to terminate a pregnancy she does not want, and to have sex if and when she desires sex, no more and no less. It is her body and her body *alone,* and she can do with it as she pleases.

A woman's self-respect, they say, cannot remain healthy if she is forced to play the role of willing and loving submission. In our society, a woman has been expected to obey her husband as she obeyed her parents, *regardless* of whether her mind might be keener, her common sense healthier, her sexual powers stronger than his. She is expected to act according to what *his image* of her is, not according to what she really is or would like to be. She is expected to mold herself after him; if their marriage is to be "strong," his will should be her own. All this is symbolized in the male expectation that she will come to the marriage bed in a virginal state—he has a "right" to her purity; the merchandise he receives should be "undamaged."

Women's Lib points out how very important it is for both partners that the woman have an identity of her own, independent of that of her man. Our society sees woman as the extension of the male—she was created from the male rib. Psychologically and socially, a woman is seen—and often sees herself—as an *incomplete* human being. Only through marriage does she gain a measure of respect and a measure of some form of dignified existence. This is reflected in the fact that the spinster in our culture is the target of endless cruel and derogatory jokes.

Emotionally, it is a grave burden for a girl to have to

affirm and reaffirm her sexual and human identity through association with a man. It must be devastating for one's self-worth, for example, to think the highlight of one's life to be the "trapping of a husband." Society should give a girl more satisfying goals than the relentless pursuit of a marriageable male. Yet many girls still go to college with this and little else in mind. No matter how young a girl may be, or how talented and intelligent and independent, once she has "caught" her man, the rest of her life, as she sees it, can be only downhill. She is considered permanently bound to this man: a servant to *his* needs, *his* sexual plaything, the mother of *his* children. After marriage, a man is expected to take charge of his life; a woman is expected to renounce any claim to a life of her own. Her major "goal" has been achieved.

Women's Lib very much objects to the demand that a woman play the role of an unreliable, witless, simpleminded child. Often, women will *choose* to be emotional rather than rational, tearful rather than reasonable, because such behavior has been rewarded in the past. Women have learned to pretend to be stupid so as not to frighten away a man. Except in childish temper tantrums, a woman is not permitted to show any justified anger or outrage—the image of a "good" woman is one who can cry easily and softly and stop when being comforted by a man's strong arms.

This wish on a man's part for the female to be childish and sweet finds its outward expression in the custom that a wife be younger than her husband, or at least *look* much younger, so as to assure that she is pliable and will not threaten his male self-esteem. Women's Lib demands that women be given their human dignity *independent* of their sexual desirability. A woman's beauty is short-lived, and is in any case something over which she has little control. There is always someone younger, someone more beautiful, or sexier, or more sly and cunning, or newer and less familiar, to take her place and compete for the affection of the male. OWL—Older Women's Liberation—is part of this general movement, protesting against having "worth" judged by standards of beauty and youth. The members point out how humiliating and unfair it is for a mature woman to have to remain "young" for a very long time. A mature woman is not permitted to take pride in her age, yet she is ridiculed for holding on to youth.

Women's Lib also asserts that the role of submission that a woman is forced to play amounts to intellectual suicide. In India in the past, in the ceremony of suttee, a woman was expected to burn herself to death on the corpse of her husband, since she had "ceased to exist" when he died. In prerevolutionary China, submission demanded that a woman bind her feet so they would never grow. In our society, a simple female mind—especially if it comes with a gorgeous, sexy body—is also seen as a flattering asset to have. A fine, concise mind in a homely body is a far less desired commodity on the marriage market than a luscious shell and an empty head—a fact to which every homely girl will testify. Both conditions—a bound mind and bound feet —can only be achieved through human suffering. It is no wonder that women begin to rebel against the tyranny of being seen as sexual objects first and human beings second.

Would it not be healthier for a loving relationship that a woman's success be her own and not a function of her mate's success? As things stand now, it works this way: if a man can afford to keep a woman in pointless luxury, his self-esteem will be enhanced and she will have the admira-

tion of the world. But if she is strong and reliable and
supports him in times of distress, both will be greatly
shamed. Both will hide her contribution as a stain on his
manhood and a poor reflection on her femininity. She will
feel worthy if he succeeds, apologetic if he doesn't. If she
is brighter than the male, she will play down her intelligence or look for a man superior to herself. A woman
standing on her own feet in marriage is an embarrassment
to her husband; if she is successful and he is not, she will feel
her success to be an "albatross" around her neck.

Both men and women would be emotionally healthier if
both would realize that a man's feelings of strength and
adequacy should not depend on the assurance that he is
manly *only* because she is weak; that he is intelligent *only*
because she pretends to be less than bright.

> "I decided on Rich by the time I was fifteen, and I could
> not let go until it was too late. He was the best-looking guy
> I could find, and he dated only beautiful girls. I guess I've
> always known I had nothing in common with him—that he
> could never satisfy my emotional needs. He had only one
> goal: to demonstrate what he could do in the sexual bed. In
> the beginning, it seemed all right—we were hungry for each
> other. But sex was simply not enough, and when I tried to
> tell him of my inner loneliness, he did not understand. His
> standard reply was: 'Don't use your fancy words on *me.*' "

It is also degrading and harmful to a man's pride to know
that female charm is a prime means used for male manipula-
tion. Yet straighter and more honest roads are often not
available to a woman. It is only through wile and cunning
that many women will gain some power over their destinies.
How this dishonesty affects the male is often reflected in our

myths. Eve was the first woman to use sex as a lure. Her longing for the "forbidden"—and man's weakness in giving in to her—cost both of them their immortality. The Bible gives several more examples of what happens when sexual cunning is directed against man. Samson and Delilah are the prime examples of how disastrous it can be when a man falls prey to the trickery of sex. Samson, the strongest man ever known, lost all his strength as a result.

History also gives many examples. Cleopatra, Helen of Troy, Jezebel, Catherine the Great of Russia, Madame de Pompadour—all used their sexual power as a means of dominating kingdoms and gaining control over men. The notion is still with us today that a very powerful woman must be sexually driven, either by unfulfilled sexual needs or by an insatiable sexual appetite. Why else would she want to rebel against the blessed state of being mistress of her home?

Women's Lib points out that in the past, sexuality in a woman has traditionally been seen as just that: a disruptive and destructive force that had to be kept under control, like a fire that could warm when contained but would destroy if left unguarded by men. Witchcraft, with its sexual overtones, is associated with being female: women having intercourse with Satan and plotting evil against the world. The harm they inflict is often portrayed to be of a sexual nature —men losing their potency, their virility, their strength. Our fairy tales portray "good" women as being blond, soft, submissive; "bad" women have dark, fiery eyes, reflecting a "passionate mind."

Those women who might come to question some of these cultural norms will find that they are very much alone. Often, if a woman shows some dissatisfaction with her lot, it will be speculated that "all she needs is a real man."

Ironically, the women in the liberation movement are often accused of being bitter and hostile and dissatisfied because they themselves have been unsuccessful in catching their men. They must be lacking in feminine charms, it is pointed out facetiously, or they would not be asking such troublesome questions. "The problem with those libbers," it is often said, "is that they have never been properly laid."

It is for the above reasons that for the first time in human history one sex has turned against the other and has declared war for the sake of emotional and intellectual survival. Women are pitted against their men, challenging the institution of marriage as being hurtful to human dignity. The women's liberation movement asserts that there is something suffocating for both men and women in the closeness and constraint that come with monogamy. They say that just as we have a choice in selecting friends, or occupations, or hobbies, or the place where we would like to live, we should be free by inalienable rights to choose our sexual partner if and when we wish, regardless of the bonds of holy matrimony.

Some of these controversial ideas are beginning to filter down to America's coming generation. Young men and women in high schools and colleges are beginning to "marry each other" with vows they have written themselves, which often contain these words: "Let there be space between our souls so that our love may breathe." There are now many young people today—especially bright, sophisticated, charming, college-educated girls—who have become somewhat wary of the wedding band. They ask themselves: "Would I really want to be married and give up my freedom and independence and individuality to a man?" They know that in spite of all good intentions, one marriage in four ends in divorce, and this number is increasing by the year. They are aware that many couples on the warpath with each other stay together only for the sake of the children or custom or convenience, and often at tremendous costs in happiness and peace of mind and dignity. In marriage, sexual joy becomes a duty by law, spontaneity becomes a drag. A boy and a girl who chose each other under the spell of romantic love discover before long that marriage can be conducive to lying and cheating and hypocrisy and loneliness, because the constraints of a lifelong union can be strangling. It is a psychic stress few people can endure without at least some compromise to their integrity.

This search of women for their independence and their true sexual identity will bring a new dimension to the relationship between the sexes. It really probes for the true essence of what sex means in a loving relationship, what it means to one's own as well as one's partner's emotional integrity. Women's Lib has brought about a revolution in sexual thinking that may well reshape our world of tomorrow. It would seem reasonable that a sexual partnership should be built on stronger psychological ground than a master-servant foundation. Marriage, if it is chosen, should be partnership rather than servitude, friendship rather than enslavement of one sex for the convenience of the other, should hold openness and trust instead of cunning and deceit.

Although these changes are very painful to our social structure right now, in the end they may well make a better world. So far, women have been undeveloped human beings: emotionally incoherent, sexually muted, intellectually stunted. We are only now beginning to face up to how extensive this damage has actually been. Women's Lib has given us a glimpse of what is yet to come. There seems to be some merit in what these libbers tell us so insistently: sex should be *part* of the richness of life, but not man's sole obsession.

11

GAYS HAVE THEIR SAY

Deviant Sexuality

Not only Women's Liberation is battling for human dignity on sexual frontiers. Gay Liberation has appeared in major cities with the slogan: "Out of the closets and into the streets!" A shocked America has witnessed something else, something that has never been witnessed before in this part of the world; men turn to men, and women turn to women, in open search of satisfying sexual loving.

Homosexuality, of course, is nothing new. Same-sex loving has always been around, but until a very few years ago, gay people were forced to stay underground because their behavior and feelings were held by most people in deepest moral contempt.

This chapter will try to define just what is "normal" sex in our world by looking at sex that is different. We have chosen homosexuality as an example of "deviant sex" because it is the best-known form of "differentness." As such, it has provoked much more attention and called for sharper condemnation than other forms of being "queer." There are many derogatory, put-down labels attached to the image of a person who is gay. "He is a homosexual" is certainly a description more emotionally loaded than the equivalent "He is a heterosexual." The label evokes a mental picture of self-hatred, restriction, lack of inner stamina, or open depravity. There are vicious jokes circulating about the tastes and preferences of "fags" or "closet queens." Many people equate homosexuality with images of oral sex in dirty public lavatories. Others are convinced that certain forms of effeminate behavior—such as hip-rolling or speaking in a high-pitched voice—are sure giveaways of a person's being gay. The image of the homosexual, as most people carry it in their minds, is that of an effeminate man —some sort of abnormal, artificial woman.

The Bible, in certain parts, is sharply condemnatory of homosexuality. Mosaic law, for example, demanded that a homosexual person be punished with death by stoning. These laws originated in times when there was a sharp division between males and females in Hebrew families. An old Hebrew prayer let the man thank God each morning for "not having created me a woman." The Biblical writings on homosexuality reflect this horror and repulsion that anyone would want to "play the female role" in intercourse.

The aim of this chapter is not to speak for or against homosexuality. It attempts to show that there are no *absolute* cutoff points in sex, that "normal" and "perverted" are arbitrary divisions with moral dimensions and have little to do with the "offensive" behavior per se.

As we have seen, it takes a lot of energy and quite a bit in terms of feelings and emotions to become coherently male or female in our Western world—to be able to fall in love with a member of the opposite sex and to develop a satisfying love relationship. The preceding chapters assumed—and presented some evidence—that a child born male is compelled to strive to become male in mind, and that a child born female has to struggle just as hard to develop a female personality. It was assumed that there *is* such a thing as being emotionally male and female, and that a well-defined "proper" sexual identity is necessary for one's inner peace of mind. And generally it is well agreed upon that "satisfying sex" means heterosexual sex—we behave "normally" only when relating to a member of the *opposite* sex. Still more specifically, "proper" sex behavior is that kind of activity where the man lies on top of the woman during intercourse. Anything different from having sex this way may very readily be labeled by some people a "perversion."

Listen to what gay people have to say:

> "There is really nothing wrong with what we do; in fact, much of it makes darn good common sense. No man can really know about the sensations in a woman's body, or the emotions in her mind. No woman could ever really know just what is pleasure for a man, and where, and for what reasons. Being gay means dealing with familiar bodies and familiar emotions. . . . Feelings are not as frightening, and therefore are easier to share. One could logically assert that there are built-in limitations between *unlike* people that are not present in a homosexual relationship."

> "Gay people experience emotional and sensual involvement that differs not at all from heterosexual love. We too enjoy being in the presence of each other, and holding hands, and kissing, and sleeping in each other's arms."

"Why would you claim that homosexuality is a childhood fixation? What is so special about just one kind of intercourse? Is that not a fixation? Besides, many straight couples make love in ways other than genital intercourse. To have straight sex and nothing else is not that privileged a deal."

"Just what is so inherently virtuous about restricting one's deepest pleasures to only half of the human race? Being homosexual—or bisexual—means being able to relate to both males and females in a loving, sexual way. Rather than it being an illness, homosexuality should be seen as an added dimension of living and loving. It means loving more broadly than society permits. It means having a certain power over ingrained and meaningless taboos. Why should it be so hard to understand that same-sex loving might be a *preference* rather than a defect in one's personality? Just who gets hurt?"

Conventional thinking will find this line of reasoning very shocking and strange. Yet the above quotations have certainly a lot to say about our image of homosexuality. For one, they call into question the common belief that gay people identify with the mentality of the opposite sex, wish to accept the role that goes with it, and often even wish for a different body. Many people think that homosexuals are in feelings the exact reverse of the sexually "normal" person—that their emotions are backward and twisted, and that they have no greater desire than to shed their uncomfortable sexual identity. This belief that a homosexual has a body that belongs to one sex and a mind and emotions that belong to the other is fueled by such sensational news stories as the much-publicized "sex change" operation of a soldier named George Jorgensen, who several years ago became convinced that in his male body there was indeed a woman trapped. This man—after costly hormonal and psychological treatment which brought him no relief—finally persuaded his doctors to let him undergo sex surgery that would give him the desired vagina and do away with his hateful male equipment. This person received much publicity as "Christine Jorgensen" later on. However, Jorgensen was not an average homosexual. In this case, we would be more correct to say that this was a *trans-sexual* personality—someone who actually crossed sexual lines. This operation, by the way, has been repeated several hundred times on other people since Jorgensen decided on sex change.

Homosexuality is something altogether different. Spokesmen of the homophile movement—in part a political movement that aims to make the public understand the nature of homosexuality—stress this.

Homos means "same"; *philos* means "loving." These Greek terms stand for *object choice, not for a mistaken identity.* Most homosexual men look like men, feel like men, talk like men, and have no desire to be anybody else. Most homosexual women look like women; they have no desire to play the role of men. *They prefer, however, to make love to a same-sex member.* They feel attracted to a same-sex person, they don't wish for a different sex. The conflict is *not* within their own identity; the conflict, as they see it, is outside in the world which stubbornly refuses to understand that some people would willingly choose to love a person who happens to have the same genital equipment that they do.

"Frank and I were buddies since grade school. We shared everything. We raced our minibikes together. We went hunting, and fishing, and swimming together. We

thought girls were the silliest creatures in this world. One
afternoon, while we sunbathed on the beach, I told him that
I loved him. It seemed a natural thing to do. I will never
forget the look on his face. He said: 'That's disgusting! Are
you out of your mind? You must be sick!' "

For the sake of a logical argument, let's detach ourselves
for a moment from the emotional aspects of this unusual
situation. Let's look at sex—all sex—by means of an
analogy.

Let's assume that a color spectrum represents all forms of
human sexual behavior. Where, on this spectrum, does
"red" stop and "yellow" begin? Which color is "normal,"
and which one is "sick"? Just where is the cutoff point for
normality? Normal versus abnormal and healthy versus sick
are matters of *degree;* this is true of all forms of sexual behavior, not just the homosexual way of love.

As an extreme example of blurred sexual borders, let's
take one form of sexual gratification which really seems out
of joint and queer. *Fetishism,* for example, is a form of sexual
behavior in which pleasure is derived in ways that seem to
have nothing to do with sex. Fetishism is sex gone astray,
so to speak. The sexual organs are of no interest at all to a
fetishist, because an "irrelevant" stimulus takes the place of
the genitals. "Pure" fetishism seems indeed strange to our
way of thinking. A shoe fetishist, for example, may secretly
collect shoes and slippers of women and hide them in his
closet, because he finds it gratifying to *look* at them while
fantasizing sexual thoughts. Other "objects" that arouse a
fetishist may be fingernails, underwear, hair, bare feet, even
disfigurations such as a hunchback or even a missing limb.
We may shake our heads at a person who stares at slippers
in a closet and becomes sexually excited as a result; yet, in

principle, how is a picture on one's nightstand all that different? It, too, is an *inanimate* thing. It, too, takes the *place* of the person. And it, too, can have the powers of sexual arousal *in the absence* of the person whom we love.

But looking at sex from a distance—and using the analogy of colors—can we not say this: red is *different* from purple, and green is *different* from pink? The color most common on our earth, let's say, is green. A color very rare is purple. Therefore we will designate that green be the "normal" color and purple the "perverted." We will assert that anyone preferring purple must be very sick indeed and must have a mixed-up color identity. Why would anyone want purple if it is well agreed upon that green is the "proper" color choice?

As a further illustration, let's look at Eskimo lovemaking. Eskimos are said to have a preference for nose-rubbing when they feel amorous. Nose-rubbing would be "normal" for Eskimos. We don't usually rub noses; we kiss. But if we should happen to rub our noses together in love play, or an Eskimo should happen to kiss, is such behavior, therefore, sick? When we say that "normal" is that which is common, and "perverted" is that which is rare, we are making a *value* assumption that all people *have* to be alike in what they prefer and practice sexually. When we say that average equals normal and deviance equals vice, we are classifying homosexuals with the same illogic with which we classify purple as a hideous color. It is very important to make this distinction when thinking about homosexuality: is a person different only *in comparison* to a group of people who happen to be alike, or is he "bad" by virtue of his isolated position on the spectrum of human sexuality? Not all people are made of the same behavioral mold.

Let's see if "normal" sex can be defined perhaps another way. Previously we said that "healthy" sex is pleasure derived from one's body, not necessarily given by a member of the opposite sex. Masturbation certainly is "normal" by the criterion of universal practice. It is, by common professional consensus, a legitimate way of finding sexual release without the help of a member of the opposite sex. When we speak of "normal" sexual behavior, do we mean pleasure through body stimulation, or do we mean pleasure that has to come according to a social prescription? If normal sex is defined as pleasure derived from one's body, then it should not greatly matter just how this pleasure is come by.

Perhaps society's rules can help us out of this dilemma. The laws in most states deal with homosexuality as a misdemeanor, sometimes even a criminal offense. But enforcement discriminates between the sexes: a woman is very rarely arrested on homosexual charges, while this is a real danger for a man. Women have far more license in what is seen as homosexual conduct. Women can hold hands in public, or embrace, or kiss affectionately. No such behavior is permitted to a man. It is far easier for two women to live together without arousing suspicion. Women can wear jeans and leather belts, or have short hair and rough shirts —a man can't even wear nylon stockings without risking raised eyebrows and snide attacks on his masculinity. It seems that as far as society goes, it is not so much the behavior per se which is offensive but who does what with whom.

Perhaps there is no such thing as *a* homosexual. Perhaps all of us are bisexual to a degree. Every normal person probably has some homosexual feelings; it simply can't be helped. It is emotionally impossible to have neutral or out-and-out hostile feelings about sexual attributes of other people whose bodies happen to be made the same way as ours. It is more nearly correct to say that there are people who *practice* homosexual acts; and some do it more often than others. But if we then try to define homosexuality by the frequency of homosexual contacts, we are not one iota nearer to the "truth." Some teen-agers try sex at first with a same-sex partner because it seems safer to do it that way. It is easier to try out sexual territory if one is unsure of just what might happen. Teen-age homosexuality is usually not taken very seriously by society; it is seen as a normal part of growing up. Society is also willing to look the other way in times of war or in situations such as imprisonment when heterosexual love is hard to come by. Some people have a homosexual experience once or twice out of curiosity and find they do not like it at all. Some prefer it occasionally, as a variation to their more common heterosexual patterns. There are some people who frequently like to swing both ways. There are a number of "happily married" people who maintain homosexual life-styles on the sly. There are others who are deeply unhappy in conventional marriages but lack the strenth to "come out" and drop the mask of pretense. And there are a small number of outspoken people who find nothing attractive in the opposite sex and make no qualms about confessing to an exclusively homosexual way of life.

Which ones of the examples above are homosexuals, and which ones are not?

All this points to one conclusion: it is simply not logically defensible to speak of homosexuality as an all-or-nothing phenomenon. It is much more logical—and makes much better common sense—to speak of a *range* of behavior where certain sexual acts may or may not be the norm.

According to homosexual spokesmen, therefore, we are dealing with attitudes in *others* that need to be changed, not with an inherent "illness" in the homosexual that has to be "cured."

> "I feel that if the outside world labels me sick, then it is up to the outside world to substantiate such claim. What is the public evidence? Can you just walk in on me and declare that my kidneys are failing, without some proof? It is not up to *me* at all to convince *you* that I think I happen to be just fine. If my body is sick, I decide when it is time to call for a doctor. Give me the same courtesy when it comes to my sexual life."

> "It makes far more sense to teach others just what homosexuality means, rather than to ask the homosexual person to 'adapt' or 'accept himself' or to learn to 'live with his differentness' or to 'change.' What is, after all, so terrible about two men making love to each other, or two women finding each other attractive in a sexual way? It is a form of relating sexually that is as old as the world. Greek and Roman classics describe homosexuality as the preferred mode of behavior; and many of our finest minds, now and in the past, are and have been proud and avowed homosexuals."

Being different is not the same as being sick. Being different, however, means having a greater chance of becoming sick as a result. Life is far easier on a heterosexual self. There are simply not as many emotional pressures on people who are straight. For example, a young homosexual individual, as a rule, has no one to identify with. Seldom does he or she know that there are many others who struggle with feelings that are different. A homosexual belongs to an "invisible minority." Other minority groups know that they can share their grievances and tribulations. Indians and Mexicans and blacks know that there are others like them with whom to share common concerns. So do old people; everyone gets old in time. Handicapped people can talk about their "differentness," confident that others will understand. A homosexual boy or girl has none of these comforts to bring some relief to the psyche, and as a rule, will feel terribly alone.

It is not so easy to live with oneself under such stress. If a whole society steps in and declares a certain person to be perverted, that is like a distorting mirror held up to one's self-respect: no matter which way you look at yourself, the image reflected back will be ugly. It is natural to come to feel unclean, unworthy, unlovable, and wicked under such massive mental assault. And it is quite a task to grow a decent self-esteem.

Since life is harder on a homosexual self, it is reasonable to expect a greater emotional toll. Just as body reserves don't last forever, there are limits to what can be borne by the psychic self. If our self-esteem is taxed severely and over a long period of time, certain mechanisms will give way. Homosexuals, therefore, are often deeply unhappy people. Most professionals agree that homosexuals have a shaky sexual identity. But to say that is *not* to say that their identity is faulty *because* it is inherent in their being homosexual; it has become so *as a result* of constant feedback telling them they are abnormal sexual human beings.

"My parents would have died if they had known. It would have cost me every single friend I ever had. Yet my lover and I were deeply committed to each other, and we wanted to tell the world. . . . If I strove to please my parents,

I betrayed my love. If I stuck to my lover, it meant losing everything I held dear. . . . It was an emotional double bind; I stood to lose out no matter which way I turned."

It has been demonstrated in the psychological laboratory that even animals will break down mentally if they have to conform to contradictory commands, to antagonistic expectations. The same is true for human beings:

"I had to be straight so as to buffer society, and I had to be gay for my own peace of mind. I felt like having membership cards in mutually antagonistic clubs—just where were my loyalties, since I had an emotional investment in both?"

It remains to be seen what will happen in our society as gay people struggle to be accepted on their own terms and under conditions they set forth. The homophile movement and its message is new and very controversial, far more so than the cry for women's rights.

12

LOVE IN TOMORROW'S WORLD

Assumptions Revisited

"What will be next?" some people moan in exasperation. Only recently, streaking became a fad. For a culture which less than a century ago had moral scruples about a bare ankle or wrist, things surely change rapidly! Ten years ago —even five years ago—it would have caused an uproar to have a naked man streak across the stage and steal the show on the Oscar awards night, visible from coast to coast on television screens in American living rooms. High school kids have streaked right in front of their astonished teachers. Airplane passengers entertained by a streaking stranger refused to press charges after the airplane had landed. Some senior citizens have even asked wistfully if "snailing" might be an acceptable substitute, since dashing nude at high speed might prove to be too strenuous for their "youthful" hearts. One broadcast reported four thousand streaking incidents on a single spring weekend. People—old and young

—took to streaking in what seemed to be an epidemic of hilarious joy. Whenever streaking is mentioned today, people smile. Given our past history of secrecy and prudishness regarding nudity, such change in attitude is astonishing indeed.

It seems to be an open admission that incredible changes regarding sexuality are well on the way to being accepted matter-of-factly. Specifically, it seems to indicate that spontaneous and lighthearted sexuality is here to stay, because we now live in a world that can constructively and healthily accept such sexual change.

The previous chapters have tried to advance the notion that our sexual identity is the result of prior learning. What we feel and what we think we *have* to feel depend on factors from *without*. These factors from without were relatively stable in the past. There was marriage, there were one's children, there were neat compartments called "male" and "female" roles, there was tradition and order and security. There was a stable frame of reference that lasted for hundreds and hundreds of years. In the very near future, there may no longer be such a stable situation.

We cannot even imagine what might be in store for our sexual selves as change comes faster and faster. This chapter will give a brief glance at what our sexual identity might look like in the future. The content of the following pages is of a highly speculative nature, for no one can know for sure just what will happen to the self as living space becomes more crowded on our tiny spaceship Earth and people try to adjust their inner gyroscopes to a very different and constantly changing world.

Some of these changes will be of such a mind-blowing nature that it can really make one's imagination spin. One of the most incredible things—looking as though it came straight from a far-out science fiction book—is the possibility of re-creating one's self by means of a process called "cloning." In cloning, the nucleus of an adult cell is artificially stimulated to reproduce itself—to create an identical organism. This has already been demonstrated with the cell nucleus of a frog. Imagine having the option of starting yourself all over again—of creating a brand-new "me"! Or, even more confusing, imagine having forty carbon copies of yourself around, all struggling to establish a sexual identity! Will we even like such an option? For as long as we can trace our civilization, it was always assumed that the psychological push behind the sexual drive was the "innate need" to reproduce. People were believed to desire sex because consciously or unconsciously they wanted children in order that they could live on in their offspring. Parental love was taken for granted because of this assumption. However, biologically a child is only half of you. The other half came from "stranger," a partner you may or may not love, may not even have loved during the very moment of procreation. Logically, one would think that cloning would be the "perfect" answer to our need for immortality. Yet people shy away from this possibility as if a monster would be created:

> "The idea is very repulsive to me. To think that someone who looks like me, talks like me, would sit next to me. . . . I don't even want to think about such nonsense. That's perverted. It's against human nature! I'm *me;* no one can take my place."

Such an option really separates sex from procreation. Is it frightening on that account? Yet much of the lesser changes to come will be in response to having sex divorced from procreation. Many people already believe that sex for its own sake will be accepted matter-of-factly in the future, even for the very young and the unmarried.

Many scientists feel that few human inventions ever made have the power to be as potentially upheaving as the Pill and other contraceptive devices. We are only now beginning to feel the enormous emotional impact of what it truly means to enjoy sex without having the sword of Damocles hanging over one's head—the fear of an unwanted pregnancy. Contraceptives have changed our whole outlook on sex.

Not long ago there appeared in a local newspaper an article which told that Latin American countries, in their attempts to combat overpopulation, were using the following slogan: "Virgin Mary, you who conceived without sinning, help us sin without conceiving." Many U.S. citizens thought this to be in very poor taste and felt strongly that such a slogan violated sacred territory. However, it is not so different a shift in attitudes from what has already occurred here in the United States. American teen-agers can freely go to birth-planning clinics and ask the *state* to help them "sin without conceiving." They will be given contraceptives and advice, without questions asked, and without their parents' permission or approval or even knowledge. Yet their parents pay taxes so that this assistance can be available. As a society, we would not approve of the use of public funds for an "immoral" purpose if we did not begin to recognize that people cannot be permitted to reproduce according to whim or greed, or by chance or ignorance, or even out of love. These birth-planning clinics are a tacit approval that "sacred" sanctions may have to be bent a little for the good of everyone involved. We are all responsible for our sexual deeds, not only to the people we know but to the larger society as well. Many professionals, therefore, believe that the realistic road to healthy sexual conduct is no longer to forbid premarital sex and close one's eyes and hope it will not happen. Pressures in teen-age life are tremendous.

> "We live in a different world. Whereas, before, virginity was an asset to be possessed, now it is a stigma to be endured. Many of us, including me, feel actually freaky for not having tried sex when everyone else is having a good time. You are pushed into this thing whether you want to or not."

Against such pressure, it seems reasonable to teach our psychological mechanism we call our "conscience" that contraception is part of responsible living, no matter how young we are, or how wise we think we are, or whether we wear a wedding band or not. Many professionals working with teen-agers feel that since teen-age sex is here to stay, contraceptives will have to become as commonplace and as matter-of-fact as brushing one's teeth each morning. Their efforts are geared to teaching the teen-age self that only a tiny part of the sexual drive is needed for procreation, and even that part may become obsolete soon. The rest must be channeled into healthy sexual activity that will not hurt the individual with guilt or society with unwanted children.

Related to this change of having sex distinct from procreation is another psychological consequence. Sex for its own sake will do away with fertility as a means of building ego strength. Population pressures may well do away with a man's testicles and a woman's uterus and ovaries, at least in the functional and symbolic sense. This will devaluate our sexual worth, according to traditional thinking.

Since time immemorial, females have relied upon the fact
that the only way a man could father a child was for him to
be united with a woman in intercourse. And males have
relied upon the fact that virility was necessary for conception. This is no longer true today. Sperm can be obtained
from an unknown donor, and can be kept frozen in a sperm
bank for very many years. What will it do to a man's ego
to know that "his" woman can simply go to a doctor's office
and have an artificial insemination—a procedure already
well in use—whereby a stranger's sperm is implanted in the
woman's uterus without the woman knowing who the father
of the baby is, or even caring? What will it do to a woman's
ego to know that it will soon be possible to grow human
embryos in laboratory jars, and that a man can go and "pur-
chase" a baby by prescription, complete with its genetic
blueprint on its wrist? We do not know.

Other unforeseen imbalances in the psychological realm
may come with the option of choosing the sex of one's
offspring—a possibility some people think is less than ten
years away. If parents can decide on the sex of their child
—instead of having it chosen for them by a "throw of dice"
—it may well be that this would result in a lopsided and
unbalanced baby crop: all boys for five years; then, as a
counter reaction, all girls for the next decade or so. Such
sexual faddishness can't help having repercussions in society. If more boys than girls are born, will that give rise to
more wars, and more crime, and less feelings, and less love?
If more girls than boys are chosen, will the result be a
whiny, clinging, dependent, emotional world? Or will people turn back to religion if women have the upper hand, or
back to frontier principles where men can carry a gun and
walk with a mighty stride? More seriously: will we vote

according to a handsome face if the constituency is mostly female, or according to dimensions such as 36-22-36 if there's a shortage in that commodity?

With these changes about to upset the male-female balance and interdependence, is it not logically possible that the very notion of maleness-femaleness will become extinct —that we will have a bisexual world? Up to present days, nothing has mattered more in human relationships than an individual's respective sex. It is the very first thing we will notice about another human being; it is the one thing we are least likely to forget. If men as well as women can have babies by simply going to a baby store, and if homosexuality becomes an accepted way of life, it may no longer matter greatly in our sexual future just who is who. Right now, we are so engrossed in sexual roles, we take these roles so much for granted, that no one seems to ask: just what causes heterosexuality? And what keeps it going? And what could make it stop?

Since sex in the future may no longer mean procreation in the traditional sense, there are now more and more people who are beginning to feel that the very concept of love will have to be modified.

> "When my mother was married to Dad, she thought naïvely that the ability to love was the most important quality a human being could possess. For me, such a vague notion is not enough. Bill and I have put down on paper our exact needs and expectations of each other, and what we will do if our needs are no longer met."

This young woman lives in a "trial marriage" with a man who agrees with her that it is essential to be superficial about love to prevent the self from being hurt. The concept of

limited loving or "loving according to contract" is one of the
more recent outgrowths of having sex distinct from procreation. The social ideal of a lifetime relationship is not appealing to many people who sense that it can be costly to the
human self to make emotional investments when the odds
are very much against people staying together for long periods of time. This is how Bill feels about his parents' love:

> "When people stayed in one place, and had to raise a
> family, it made sense to grow deep roots and form lasting
> relationships, and guard them jealously against outside in-
> trusion, and call it love. Today we are constantly on the
> move. It is no longer to my advantage to grow roots of
> attachment to another human being, knowing that three or
> five or ten years from now my needs will have changed, or
> someone else may come along who can better fulfill my
> needs."

Most forms of trial marriage are based on the assumption
that sexual relationships are interchangeable, and that the
more involved a relationship is, the greater are the pressures
on the self to fulfill each other's expectations rather than
one's own:

> "Sheila and I have a half-year contract which we have
> renewed so far five times. We reevaluate it periodically, and
> each time we specify exactly the extent of our involvement
> —who gives what, and for what reasons. . . . We will split
> without regret when our arrangement no longer makes
> sense."

Other people, however, do not agree at all that limited
loving and freedom go together. They argue that one cannot squander oneself in noncommittal sex without an inner

emotional toll, and that therefore even modern love should be lasting and meaningful. They feel that as outer space becomes more crowded, people will turn inward and explore deeper and deeper the human capacity for sexual love, and that sex will lose some of its ugliness and competitiveness as a result and will become more tender and aesthetic and spiritual.

There is a third group of people who look at loving in a still different light. They say that it is time to face up to the fact that even though love may be magic and sweet in the eyes of the beholder, looked at critically, much of it is just plain silly and make-belief. Therefore they feel it rests on an unsound and shaky psychological foundation.

> "Romantic love was always assumed to be good for the human psyche. No one ever seriously set out to prove it to be so. Certainly romantic love is artificial in many ways. . . . Look at how accidentally we fall in love, and how foolishly we behave when in love, and how we keep on hurting and cheating and lying, all in the name of love, and what an awful aftertaste so-called love can leave. Perhaps we have asked the impossible of sexual love; perhaps it is time to call a spade a spade."

There are now several books on the market that actually teach lovers how to fight. Their message is that tender feelings can be killed by an overdose of sweetness, and that there is nothing healthier for the human self than an occasional premeditated, well-aimed pie smashed across the face of one's lover.

In all of the above, however, there is one implicit assumption: that in a modern world, love per se can no longer be used as a blanket guarantee for happiness, and that the modern self has to make adjustments to the reality of impermanence and change.

This book was written for this very reason. We need to know ourselves; we badly need to know what happens in the realm of sexual emotions. This book was meant to give a kaleidoscopic glimpse of current psychological thinking, to give readers some knowledge, some awareness of the dynamics involved in human sexuality. Some of what is known about the human self psychologists have learned through hard, rigorous, systematic experimentation. Much of their knowledge is still incomplete. Some is speculation. Perhaps a tiny bit is even superstition. Psychologists, dealing with a brand-new science, really have more questions than answers at this point. The self itself, as it was scrutinized and dissected in this book, is a *construct* some people feel may or may not exist.

Emotions, or whatever it is that we feel, do exist, however. As we step into tomorrow's world, we need to know about these feelings. We also need to realize that things look different from different points of view. There are hidden forces coming from without that push us here and there, into disaster perhaps if we are not aware. There are needs within ourselves and needs within the persons whom we love that have a powerful say for our futures. There is so much that could be said about causation in our world, and about our freedom to handle what comes our way and hooks on to our emotions and won't let go. There is a world to discover about the science of human behavior. For a beginning, isn't it worth the trouble to back up a little and look with curiosity at our sexual selves and be awed?